Ready-to-U

VIOLENCE PREVENTION SKILLS
LESSONS &
ACTIVITIES

for Elementary Students

 RUTH WELTMANN BEGUN
and
FRANK J. HUML, **Editors**

THE SOCIETY FOR PREVENTION OF VIOLENCE *with*
THE CENTER FOR APPLIED RESEARCH IN EDUCATION

THE CENTER FOR APPLIED
RESEARCH IN EDUCATION
West Nyack, New York 10994

Library of Congress Cataloging-in-Publication Data

Ready-to-use violence prevention skills, lessons & activities for
    elementary students / Ruth Weltmann Begun and Frank J. Huml, editors;
    the Society for Prevention of Violence with the Center for Applied
    Research in Education.
            p.   cm.
        Includes bibliographical references.
        ISBN 0–87628–136–6
        1. School violence—Prevention—Study and teaching (Elementary)
    2. Conflict management—Study and teaching (Elementary)   I. Begun,
    Ruth Weltmann.   II. Huml, Frank J.   III. Society for Prevention of
    Violence (Ohio)   IV. Center for Applied Research in Education.
    LB3013.3.R43   1999
    371.7'82—dc21   99–30609
                                                                              CIP

© 1999 *by* The Society for Prevention of Violence, Cleveland, Ohio

Printed in the United States of America

10 9 8 7 6 5 4 3 2 1

ISBN 0-87628-136-6

**THE CENTER FOR APPLIED RESEARCH
IN EDUCATION**
West Nyack, NY 10994

On the World Wide Web at http://www.phdirect.com

ABOUT THIS VIOLENCE PREVENTION SKILLS
TEACHING RESOURCE

Today's educators carry added responsibilities because significant social changes have had an impact on human relations. Family ties have been loosened. The number of single-parent families has grown. Stresses in many families are often high. Thus, young people are frequently exposed to influences that tend to make them aggressive and possibly violent. Moreover, television, now in almost every home in the United States, frequently shows events not suitable for guiding our young. Juveniles who cannot read and write watch violent scenes and might draw wrong conclusions. Children are very adept with computers and thus are able to surf the Internet for programs not suitable for their age. Unless schools, other social agencies, and parents counteract the media and other asocial influences using preventive means, verbal and physical interpersonal abuse and violence will be an increasing problem.

This resource is one of two books in the "Ready-to-Use Violence Prevention Skills Lessons & Activities Library" to help parents, teachers and other caregivers to acquaint children with dangerous situations that they might face and to teach them how to cope with such dangers and to resolve them peacefully.

The full library spans all grade levels and includes:

▶ Ready-to-Use Violence Prevention Skills, Lessons & Activities for Elementary Students
▶ Ready-to-Use Violence Prevention Skills, Lessons & Activities for Secondary Students

This volume is designed to be used by teachers, parents, and other adults dealing with children of an elementary age. It is meant to be a companion to the four-volume series entitled "Ready-to-Use Social Skills Lessons & Activities" developed by The Society for Prevention of Violence. It contains forty-four (44) lessons and about ninety (90) associated activity worksheets focusing on topics such as stimulant use, family relationships, dealing with anger, and crime-related topics. These contemporary subject matters are well suited to today's classroom.

The lessons are presented in a uniform format and follow a Structured Learning Approach to teach the skills. They focus on real situations in children's own lives, such as dealing with feelings, recognizing stress and danger situations, learning to cope with depression and loneliness, and comprehending the harm caused by stimulant use and criminal behavior, and are readily adapted to teaching in any classroom, school, or home setting.

The ideas, stories, and scenarios for most of the lessons and activities are concerned with violence in the family, drug abuse, alcohol abuse, juvenile crime, psychology, social skills, and conflict resolution. This volume, for use with elementary students, serves as a companion to the volume for secondary students and follows the same format. The project was funded by The Society for Prevention of Violence, a non-profit organization founded by the late Semi J. Begun, Ph.D. and his wife, Ruth Weltmann Begun, M.S., and sponsored by them and various contributing corporations and foundations, including the Semi J. and Ruth W. Begun Foundation. Specific credits to advisors and consultants are given on the Acknowledgments page.

Major objectives of teaching these lessons are to build students' character and help them develop the understanding and skills necessary to deal with difficult and violence-threatening situations in ways that lead to settlement of conflicts and grievances through communication without recourse to violence. I believe that such training can be effective and successful by preventing the use of violence. Thus, students will benefit from the practice of violence prevention skills throughout their lives.

Ruth Weltmann Begun, M.S.
The Society for Prevention of Violence

ACKNOWLEDGMENTS

This curriculum, serving as a companion to the four-volume "Ready-to-Use Social Skills Lessons & Activities" series, was developed under the direction of Ruth Weltmann Begun, President, and Frank J. Huml, previous Executive Director, of The Society for Prevention of Violence. The following persons served as advisors and consultants to the project:

Juanita Flinner, previous Assistant to the Executive Director, The Society for Prevention of Violence

Jane Sembric, Executive Director, The Society for Prevention of Violence

Byron Wasko, Assistant Principal, East Cleveland City School Disctrict, Ohio

Their expertise provided contributions to the content of the lessons. The editors are sincerely appreciative of their willingness to serve and contribute to the development of this companion teaching resource.

The Society is also appreciative of the continued cooperation of Mr. Winfield Huppuch, Vice President, Prentice Hall Direct.

ABOUT THE SOCIETY FOR PREVENTION OF VIOLENCE (SPV)

The Society for Prevention of Violence (SPV) is dedicated to reducing the prevalence of violent acts and asocial behaviors in children and adults through education. It accomplishes this mission by teaching children and adults the use of the skills necessary to build their character, helping them acquire a strong values system, motivating them to develop their communication skills and to realize growth in interpersonal relationships. The mission includes integration of social and academic skills to encourage those who use them to reach their full potential and contribute to our nation's society by being able to make decisions and solve problems through effective and appropriate means.

As a non-profit organization, the Society had its origin in 1972 as The Begun Institute for The Study of Violence and Aggression at John Carroll University (Cleveland, Ohio). A multitude of information was gathered, studied, and analyzed during the ensuing ten-year period. Symposia were held which involved numerous well-known presenters and participants from various career fields. Early on, the founders of the Institute, S. J. and Ruth Begun, foresaw the trend of increasing violence in our families, communities, and across the nation, and chose to take a leadership role in pioneering an educational approach to help alleviate aggressive and antisocial behavior. The educational approach was and continues to be the sole *PROACTIVE* means to change behaviors. Current conditions reflect our society's reliance on reactive means of dealing with this problem. During the next ten-year period, through the determination and hard work of Ruth Weltmann Begun as executive director, the workshops, parent training sessions, collaborative projects, and a comprehensive (preschool through grade 12) Social Skills Training Curriculum were developed.

As a follow up, a new two-volume set entitled "Ready-to-Use Violence Prevention Skills Lessons & Activities" for elementary and secondary students was prepared.

Today, classroom teachers in numerous school districts across the country are utilizing this internationally recognized curriculum. The Society continually seeks support through individual donors, grants, direct paid services, and material/consultant service sales. It also has expanded its involvement in the educational process by:

▶ publishing a semiannual newsletter, a resource catalog, and other pertinent material;

▶ providing in-service training for professional staffs of schools, parents and others;

▶ providing assistance in resource identification, proposal writing/project design and evaluation;

▶ tailoring instructional (academic and other) delivery designs to specific school/organization needs;

▶ implementing pilot demonstration projects with foundation support;

▶ offering graduate level workshops in cooperation with and through John Carroll, Kent State, and Ashland Universities in the area of teacher training (credits earned in these workshops may be applied toward renewal of certificates through the Ohio Department of Education);

▶ presentation of professional workshops for graduate credit, such as: Teaching Social Skills in the Classroom, Violence Through the Ages, Classroom Management, Gangs, Guns, Drugs and Violence, Domestic Violence, Family Dynamics, etc.;

▶ offering a graduate level credit "self-study" workshop, *Teaching Social Skills in the Classroom*, in cooperation with Ashland University (OH) to non-Ohio residents nationwide; and

▶ continued development of new workshops and other related and pertinent projects.

As we enter the twenty-first century, we must work diligently and cooperatively to turn challenges into success.

For further information, contact The Society for Prevention of Violence, 3439 West Brainard Road #206, Woodmere, Ohio 44122 (phone 216/591-1876) or 3109 Mayfield Road, Cleveland Heights, Ohio 44118 (phone 216/371-5544/45).

ABOUT THE VIOLENCE PREVENTION SKILLS CURRICULUM

Philosophy

We believe that the learning of certain life skills is the foundation for social and academic adequacy. It assists in the prevention of asocial behavior and leads to successful functioning and survival skills for our citizens. Social behavior and academic behavior are highly correlated. We believe it is more productive to teach youth the proper ways to behave than to admonish them for improper behavior. This requires direct and systematic teaching, taking into consideration social and developmental theory in the affective, cognitive, and psycho-motor domains. Learning should be sequential, linked to community goals, and consistent with behaviors that are relevant to student needs. This violence prevention skills curriculum is based on these beliefs and is closely associated in concept and format with the comprehensive preK-12 Social Skills Lessons and Activities curriculum developed by The Society for Prevention of Violence and published by Prentice Hall.

Curriculum Overview

As young people mature, one way they learn social and peaceful behaviors is by watching and interacting with other people. Some who have failed to learn appropriate behaviors have lacked opportunities to imitate good role models, have received insufficient or inappropriate reinforcement, or have misunderstood adequate social experiences.

The last decade has presented great challenges to young people and classroom teachers alike. The prevalence of weapons, drugs, alcohol, and ever-increasing family disintegration along with the reduced influence of the community-at-large have contributed to increased anti-social behaviors on the part of juveniles.

The teaching of violence prevention skills is particularly important at the elementary level. It is in these early grades that youngsters begin to develop and practice skills and behaviors that will remain with them through their teens and later years. It is particularly crucial that appropriate responses to life's challenges be learned prior to teen years because of the rapid increase in asocial behavior during these years and the significantly higher juvenile crime rates compared with other age groups that persist.

The Violence Prevention Skills Lessons and Activities curriculum closely resembles the Social Skills Lessons and Activities curriculum developed by the Society in its format, lesson structure, and philosophy. It is intended that this curriculum will be utilized as a complement to the social skills curriculum. The curriculum is designed to provide real-life situations for students to react to by using suggested skill components and by role playing and teacher modeling of the skills. The teacher and the rest of the class then provide positive reinforcement to encourage the continued use of the appropriate skills in situations that will occur in any environment.

This elementary volume serves as a companion to the secondary volume, grades 7–12. The lessons and activities in this volume are followed by a special section entitled "Social Skills Family Training Booklet." The Booklet is addressed to parents, and single pages may be copied as needed for use with individual children. The booklet includes a brief introduction to its purposes and acknowledgment to its originators followed by a family social skills checklist, and helpful hints and reminders for using the booklet and teaching social skills effectively. The heart of the booklet is comprised of "Fourteen Selected Social Skills" with suggested skill activities that can be done within the family.

Teachers using this curriculum can be flexible. The curriculum is designed to be used in the classroom as lessons taught for about 20–30 minutes, two or three times a week. However, it is not the intent that these be the only times violence prevention skills are taught and learned. Every opportunity should be used to reinforce, model, and coach the youngsters so that they can practice the skills often enough to feel comfortable with them as part of their ways of thinking and behaving. Therefore, the teacher should remind the students of the skills and the need to use them in all appropriate situations once the skills have been demonstrated. The teacher should also plan to model the skills in any and all interactions with the youngsters. The teacher should be *consistent* in not only using the skills when they are taught, but in using them in all interactions with the students. Only this kind of consistent modeling will assure that the youngsters will see the skills used repeatedly and begin to know and feel comfortable with using them. Teachers should also adapt the material to class needs and design and develop strategies, models, and interventions other than those suggested here. Students can even be involved in helping to develop modeling strategies and other techniques.

Structured Learning consists of *four basic components:* modeling, role playing, discussion of performance, and use in real-life situations. For more effective teaching, the lessons include eight steps that follow a directed lesson format (see below):

Behavioral Objective: The expected outcome of learning the violence prevention skill that can be evaluated.

Directed Lesson: Each behavior is defined and stated in observable terms; the behavior is demonstrated and practiced; a student's level of performance is evaluated and inappropriate behaviors are corrected. Positive reinforcement is used to encourage continued use of the skill in all areas of the student's environment.

1. *Establish the Need:* The purpose of teaching the lesson is included. What benefits will learning the skill provide? What are the consequences of not learning the behavior?

2. *Introduction:* Stories, charts, and questions are used to make the violence prevention skills more concrete to the children.

3. *Identify the Skill Components:* These skill steps are used to teach the behavior. By following and practicing these steps, the student will be able to demonstrate the behavior when needed.

4. *Model the Skill:* The teacher or socially adept child demonstrates the appropriate behaviors so that the students can imitate them. The skill components are referred to during the modeling.

5. *Behavioral Rehearsal:* The children are given an opportunity to perform the behavior which can be evaluated, corrected, and reinforced.

    A. *Selection*—The teacher selects participants or asks for volunteers. The number of children depends on the time allowed and whatever is appropriate for each lesson.

    B. *Role Play*—The participants are assigned their roles or situations they will role play.

    C. *Completion*—This is a means to determine that the role playing is complete. After each role play, reinforce correct behaviors, identify inappropriate behaviors, and re-enact role play with corrections. If there are no corrections, role play is complete.

    D. *Reinforcers*—Positive reinforcement by the teacher and the class is used for maintenance of the skill. Various methods can be used: verbal encouragement, tangible rewards, special privileges, and keeping a record of social and academic improvement.

    E. *Discussion*—The student's level of performance is evaluated and inappropriate behaviors are corrected. How did the participants feel while performing? What difficulties might be faced in implementing the skill? What observations did the class make?

6. ***Practice:*** Activities that help the children summarize the skill. The practice can be done by using worksheets, doing art projects, making film strips, writing stories, keeping diaries and charts, and so on.

7. ***Independent Use:*** Activities that help facilitate the use of these behaviors outside the school environment. Family and friends take an active role in reinforcing the importance of using these alternative behaviors in a conflict situation.

8. ***Continuation:*** At the end of each lesson, the teacher reminds the class that applying these skills can benefit them in academic and social relationships. Stress that although there are difficulties in applying the skills (such as in regard to negative peer pressure), the benefits outweigh the problems. One such benefit is more self-confidence in decision-making. Maintaining social behavior is an ongoing process. It requires teachers to show appropriate behaviors and reinforce them when they are demonstrated.

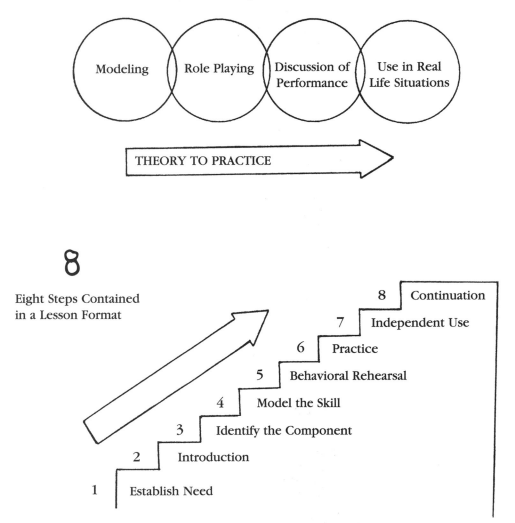

We believe that such training can be effective and successful by increasing understanding and the development of appropriate thought processes and skills to avoid conflict which might result in violence in the students' lives.

BIBLIOGRAPHY

Apter, Stephen J. & Goldstein, Arnold P. (1986). *Youth Violence: Program and Prospects*. Needham Heights, MA: Allyn & Bacon.

Barnett, O. W. & LaViolette, A. D. (1993). *It Could Happen to Anyone, Why Battered Women Stay*. Thousand Oaks, CA: Sage Publications.

Bart, P. B. & Moran, E. G. (eds.) (1993). *Violence Against Women*. Thousand Oaks, CA: Sage Publications.

Begun, Ruth Weltmann (1995). *Ready-to-Use Social Skills Lessons and Activities*, grades pre-K. West Nyack, NY: Center for Applied Research in Education.

Begun, Ruth Weltmann (1995). *Ready-to-Use Social Skills Lessons and Activities*, grades 1-3. West Nyack, NY: Center for Applied Research in Education.

Begun, Ruth Weltmann (1995). *Ready-to-Use Social Skills Lessons and Activities*, grades 4-6. West Nyack, NY: Center for Applied Research in Education.

Buzawa, E. & Buzawa, C. G. (1996). *Domestic Violence*. Thousand Oaks, CA: Sage Publications.

Byers, G. H. (1994). *Collaborative Discipline for At-Risk Students*. West Nyack, NY: The Center for Applied Research in Education.

Cartledge, Gwendolyn & Milburn, Joanne F. (1986). *Teaching Social Skills to Children*, 2nd ed. Needham Heights, MA: Allyn & Bacon.

Charles, C. M. (1989). *Building Classroom Discipline*. NY: Longman.

DeJong, W. (1994). *Preventing Interpersonal Violence Among Youth, An Introduction to School, Community, and Mass Media Strategies*. Washington DC: U. S. Department of Justice.

Edel, W. (1995). *Gun Control*. Westport, CT: Praeger Publishers.

Elias, M. J. & Tobias, S. E. (1996). *Social Problem Solving*. New York, NY: Guilford Press.

Fox, R. E. (1996). *Harvesting Minds*. Westport, CT: Praeger Publishers.

Frances, R. J. & Miller, S. I. (eds.) (1991). *Clinical Book of Addictive Disorders*. New York, NY: Guilford Press.

Frank, I. C. (1996). *Building Self-Esteem in At-Risk Youth*. Westport, CT: Praeger Publishers.

Furlong, M. J. & Smith, D. C. (1994). *Anger, Hostility and Aggression*. Brandon, VT: Clinical Psychology Publishing Co., Inc.

Gelles, R. J. & Cornell, C. P. (1990). *Intimate Violence in Families*. Thousand Oaks, CA: Sage Publications.

Gesell, Arnold, Frances L. Ilg, & Louise Bates Ames. (1977). *The Child from Five to Ten*. rev. ed. NY: Harper & Row.

Ginott, Haim. *Between Parent & Child*. (1956). NY: Avon Books.

Goldstein, Arnold P. (1991). *Delinquent Gangs*. Champaign, IL: Research Press.

Bibliography

Goldstein, Arnold P., Apter, Stephen J. & Harootunian, Berj (1984). *School Violence*. Englewood Cliffs, NJ: Prentice Hall.

Goldstein, Arnold P. et al. (1980). *Skillstreaming the Adolescent: A Structured Learning Approach to Teaching Prosocial Skills*. Champaign, IL: Research Press.

Goldstein, Arnold P. & Conoley, J. C. (1997). *School Violence Prevention*. New York, NY: Guilford Press.

Goldstein, Arnold P., Harootunian, B. & Conoley, J. C. (1995). *Student Aggression, Prevention, Management and Replacement Training*. New York, NY: Guilford Publications.

Goldstein, Arnold P., Reagles, K. W. & Amann, L. L. (1990). *Refusal Skills*. Champaign, IL: Research Press.

Hampton, R. L., Jenkins, P. & Gullotta, T. P. (eds.) (1995). *Preventing Violence in America*. Thousand Oaks, CA: Sage Publications.

Hanson, D. J. (1996). *Alcohol Education*. Westport, CT: Praeger Publishers.

Hoffman, Allen M. (ed.) (1996). *Schools, Violence and Society*. Westport, CT: Praeger Publishers.

Holinger, P. C., Offer, D., Barter, J. T. & Bell, C. C. (1994). *Suicide and Homicide Among Adolescents*. New York, NY: Guilford Press.

Huff, C. R. (ed.) (1996). *Gangs in America*. Thousand Oaks, CA: Sage Publications.

Kegan, Robert. (1982). *The Evolving Self*. Cambridge, MA: Harvard University Press.

Kirk, W. G. (1993). *Adolescent Suicide*. Champaign, IL: Research Press.

Lal, S. R., Lal, D. & Achilles, C. M. (1993). *Handbooks on Gangs in Schools*. Thousand Oaks, CA: Corwin Press.

Mannix, D. (1989). *Be a Better Student: Lessons and Worksheets for Teaching Behavior Management in Grades 4-9*. West Nyack, NY: The Center for Applied Research in Education.

Mannix, D. (1991). *Life Skills Activities for Special Children*. West Nyack, NY: Center for Applied Research in Education.

Mannix, D. (1993). *Social Skills Activities for Special Children*. West Nyack, NY: Center for Applied Research in Education.

McGinnis, E. & Goldstein, A. P. (1984). *Skillstreaming the Elementary School Child: A Guide for Teaching Prosocial Skills*. Champaign, IL: Research Press.

Morley, E. & Rossman, S. B. (eds.) (1996, August). *Education and Urban Society*. Thousand Oaks, CA: Corwin Press.

Nastasi, B. K & DeZolt, D. M. (1994). *Schools Interventions for Children of Alcoholics*. New York, NY: Guilford Press.

Pagliaro, A. M. & Pagliaro, L. A. (1996). *Substance Use Among Children and Adolescents*. New York, NY: Wiley.

Patterson, G. R. (1975). *Families*. Champaign, IL: Research Press.

Peled, E., Jaffe, P. G. & Edleson, J. L. (eds.) (1995). *Ending the Cycle of Violence—Community Responses to Children of Battered Women.* Thousand Oaks, CA: Sage Publications, Inc.

Pernanen, K. (1991). *Alcohol in Human Violence.* New York, NY: Guilford Press.

Petersen, S. & Straub, R. L. (1992). *School Crisis Survival Guide.* West Nyack, NY: The Center for Applied Research in Education.

Pfeffer, C. R. (1986). *The Suicidal Child.* New York, NY: Guilford Press.

Pirtle, Sarah. (1989). *Discovery Sessions: How Teachers Create Opportunities to Build Cooperation & Conflict Resolution Skills in Their K-8 Classrooms.* Greenfield, MA: Franklin Mediation Services Booklet.

Poland, S. (1989). *Suicide Intervention in the Schools.* New York, NY: Guilford Press.

Reiss, D., Richters, J. E., Radke-Yarrow, M. & Scharff, D. (eds.) (1993). *Children and Violence.* New York, NY: Guilford Press.

Silverman, M. M. & Maris, R. W. (1995). *Suicide Prevention.* New York, NY: Guilford Press.

Stephens, R. (1995). *Safe Schools: A Handbook for Violence Prevention.* Bloomington, IN: National Educational Service.

Stephens, R. D., Exec. Director (1990). *Gangs in Schools.* Malibu, CA: National School Safety Center.

Stephens, T. M. (1978). *Social Skills in the Classroom.* Columbus, OH: Cedars Press, Inc.

Walters, C. D. (1994). *Drugs and Crime in Lifestyle Perspective.* Thousand Oaks, CA: Sage Publications.

Wheeler, E. D. & Baron, S. A. (1994). *Violence in Our Schools, Hospitals and Public Places.* Ventura, CA: Pathfinder Publishing.

Wieke, V. R. & Richards, A. L. (1995). *Intimate Betrayal.* Thousand Oaks, CA: Sage Publications.

CONTENTS

VIOLENCE PREVENTION SKILLS LESSONS AND ACTIVITIES FOR ELMENTARY STUDENTS

Contents

Contents

SOCIAL SKILLS FAMILY TRAINING BOOKLET / 200

VIOLENCE PREVENTION SKILLS LESSONS AND ACTIVITIES FOR ELEMENTARY STUDENTS

TO THE TEACHER

This section presents forty-four (44) ready-to-use violence prevention lessons with a variety of related activities and worksheets. Some of these lessons may require more than one teaching session.

The lessons may be used in any order you desire, though they are sequenced in a broad way, beginning with general strategies for everyday life. Ultimately, of course, you will match the needs and ability levels of your student with the particular lessons and learning objectives. It may be necessary to repeat some of the lessons several times over the course of the school year.

The worksheets accompanying these lessons may be photocopied as many times as you need them for use with individual student, small groups, or the whole class. You may also devise activity sheets of your own to enrich and reinforce any of the lessons.

Violence in Our Society

Crime and violence have become commonplace in our society. The last decade has seen significant increase in juvenile violence. Such increases can only portend our future as a nation. In spite of our leadership in technological and scientific areas, we have not demonstrated the same understanding and acceptance of responsibility in addressing the needs of our youth.

- 3.6 million persons in our population are addicted to drugs

- The arrest rate for violent juveniles is expected to nearly double from current levels in the years ahead.

- 83% of juvenile detention center inmates reported owning a gun as did 22% of students attending high schools in urban areas.

- Urban schools have chronic gang problems, and suburban areas have emerging gang presence.

- Suicide rates of children are increasing.

All too often, we have approached problems of violence through legislation rather than education. Tempting as it might be to seek a simple, perhaps even curable biological cause, a large body of evidence points to violence as a learned behavior. From the earliest ages, children learn by observation, practice, and continual reinforcement.

It is important to note, that while elementary students may not involve themselves directly in violent actions, certain behaviors often portend violence in the future. Such behaviors as anger, retreat, belligerence, inability to focus, and, often, lack of acceptable social skills are directly related to socially unacceptable behavior, lack of success in life, and violence in one's relationships and/or oneself. As primary and upper elementary teachers, it is prudent to engage students in the many activities contained herein and also to teach these lessons in conjunction with the quality lessons contained in the Social Skills Lessons & Activities series.

The adage "An ounce of prevention is worth a pound of cure" holds true to this day. Our success, as educators, in most part will be measured in how well we prepare our young generation academically and *socially*.

Helping Youth Unlearn Asocial Behaviors

The school's role in combating, and preventing, violence can be a powerful one: helping young people unlearn aggression and asocial behaviors by substituting constructive learnings about cooperation, caring, understanding, and social skills for solving problems. A former surgeon general stressed that we must take an interdisciplinary approach to reducing violence. Among her prescriptions for violence prevention are incorporating violence prevention into the school curricula through teaching social skills. Resilient youth usually possess the four attributes of social competence, problem solving skills, autonomy, and a sense of purpose and future.

It is important to realize that the teaching of social skills is a primary prevention program which targets entire populations of youth in the development of skills that reduce the probability of the initial onset of problems. Such learnings are of prime importance and longest lived in terms of a continuum of prevention which also includes secondary and tertiary approaches.

Training for Life

The violence prevention skills curriculum, in this volume, closely parallels in structure, format, and methodology the curriculum in the companion four-volume Social Skills Lessons and Activities series. Primary elements of each lesson include modeling (the skill is presented by an adult role model), role play (behavioral rehearsal or practice for future use of the skill), and performance feedback (praise, approval, and encouragement are given for the appropriate display of the target skill). Topics related to substance abuse (drugs, alcohol), weapons, psychological problems, and family harmony are presented in ready-to-use lessons which can be supplemented/enhanced in many ways by the creative teacher.

These lessons become universal life skills training. For many schools, the addition of social skills and prevention programming may seem to be another "drain" on the teacher's day. Yet elementary and secondary educators, and key adults in the community (social service agencies, parent groups, outreach groups, and religious groups), are the first line of defense in our nations attempt to curb violence.

We believe that the use of this material can be effective and successful in improving discipline, reducing the dropout rate, and teaching youth to cope with adverse feelings in a peaceful manner. Thus, students will benefit from violence prevention skills as well as from related training such as teaching of social and other life skills throughout their lives.

Coping with Difficulties in Life

Behavioral Objective: Students will learn that using Social Skills might make it possible for them to cope with serious difficulties. In some cases, they have to understand the necessity for changing friendships, which requires courage, conviction, and the appreciation of social values.

Directed Lesson:

1. **Establish the Need:** Children yearn, as do adults, for attention, love, and belonging. In this process of yearning, they frequently join up with friends who have no appreciation of society's values, rules and regulations. In some cases, those friends might even go as far as stealing, threatening, hurting, and maybe killing. Once they have joined such a group, children find it difficult to break away and make new friends. Children will learn that acquiring social skills and other life skills will make it easier for them to find friends who are better adjusted to their environment.

2. **Introduction:** The teacher will read the following story to the class:

   One morning, just before school started, two boys, William, age 8, and Jeffrey, age 9, got into a big fight with one another. The two students were immediately taken to the principal's office. After letting the students calm down, the principal wanted to know "Who started the fight and why?"

   Jeffrey just sat there looking very angry and refused to say anything about the fight, but William said that he had had enough and that he was going to tell everything.

   He told about always "hanging out" with the same group of boys that constantly got into trouble. This group would go into stores or homes and steal things. They also would make threats and beat up kids if they didn't give them their money.

   One time William was with this group of boys when they decided to rob another boy of his new tennis shoes. When the boy wouldn't give them his tennis shoes, Andrew and Jeffrey beat and kicked the boy so badly that there was blood everywhere. At that point, William knew that if he didn't get away from this group of boys, he would end up lying in a pool of his own blood.

   He told the principal that he wanted to change his life, but he did not know how to go about it. The principal recommended that he have a talk with the guidance counselor.

   The teacher will ask the following questions:

   ▶ **What will the guidance counselor suggest?**

   ▶ **What are social skills?**

3. ***Identify the Skill Components:*** List the following skill components on the board or on sentence strips:

1. Consider the situation.

2. Realize that you alone are responsible.

3. Decide how to account to yourself.

4. Think what you want to do.

5. Decide how you could get out of the situation.

6. Ask for help if needed.

7. Make a wise decision.

4. ***Model the Skill:*** The teacher will select a student to play the role of William from the story in the introduction. Using the skill components, the teacher will role play and guide William through the process of how to cope with life's difficulties by using social skills.

5. ***Behavioral Rehearsal:***

   A. *Selection:* The teacher will select appropriate numbers of students to role play.

   B. *Role Play:* The teacher will ask students to role play the following situations. (The scenarios can be written on index cards or explained orally to the role players.)

      – You are with a group of students who are about to rob another student of his/her money. The student refuses to give them his/her money.

      – You are with a group of students when one of the students takes out a toy gun from his/her book bag. The group decides to go about scaring other people by pointing the gun at them.

      – You are with a group of students when one of the group takes out a pack of cigarettes and tells everyone "Let's smoke!"

   C. *Completion:* After each role play, the teacher will reinforce correct behavior, identify inappropriate behavior, and have the children re-enact the role play with corrections if necessary. If there are no corrections, the role play is complete.

   D. *Discussion:* The teacher will begin the discussion by asking the children about responsibility and accountability. The teacher will then lead a discussion about the skill components and how they can be applied to many situations.

6. ***Practice:*** The teacher will have students complete the worksheet "In Trouble!" and share their responses in class.

7. ***Independent Use:*** Distribute the worksheet "Serious Difficulties." Ask students to return the completed worksheet in one week and discuss their responses in class.

8. ***Continuation:*** The teacher will use every opportunity to tell the children that he/she is always available to help if they feel that they are in serious difficulties and that social skills can be helpful to get them out of the most serious troubles when they apply them correctly.

Name _____ Date _____

"In Trouble"

Directions: Write a couple of sentences telling about two difficulties that you had with other students, what you did then and how you would handle each situation now, using the skill components.

DIFFICULTY

1. _____

_____

2. _____

_____

How I solved it then . . .

1. _____

_____

2. _____

_____

How I would handle the difficulty now . . .

1. _____

_____

_____

2. _____

_____

_____

Did you use the Skill Components?

Yes _____   No _____

Name _____ Date _____

Serious Difficulties

Directions: Talk to your parent, grandparent, or friend about some difficulties they experienced and list their solutions and how they got out of these difficulties. Also list how you would handle these same difficulties by using the skill components.

Difficulty	Solution as Told	Solution by You with Use of Skill Components

Learning to Value Life

Behavioral Objective: Students will learn that life has special value and nobody has the right to destroy anything that is living.

Directed Lesson:

1. **Establish the Need:** Children, of today, have become desensitized to loss of life because they see life being destroyed in seconds and by the will of others in films, cartoons, video games, and on TV. Some children have even witnessed people of all ages lose their lives to violence and feel that they, too, will die before they become adults. And the violence and loss of life is not confined to people. Frequently animals are treated cruelly, maimed and killed "just for fun." Children need to learn to respect and value life in order to make the world safer and happier.

2. **Introduction:** The teacher will relate the following story to the class:

   Sammy had always enjoyed watching action cartoons with many scenes in which the characters get "blown away," only to be back in a new episode the next week or in a new movie.

   When Sammy was about ten years old, he and his twin sister decided to find out if it was really possible to send something up into the sky on a rocket and if it would return shortly. (He'd seen this many times in cartoons.) He knew where his dad had put some leftover fireworks and selected several rocket-type pieces. He knew whatever he sent up on the rockets could not weigh too much because these were small fireworks, so he decided to use his brother's pet, a hamster. Fortunately for the hamster, Sammy was stopped before he could light the rockets.

   The teacher will ask the following questions:

   ▶ **Was Sammy permitted and was it safe to play with leftover fireworks?**

   ▶ **What do you think would have happened to the hamster if Sammy had lighted the rocket?**

   ▶ **What could have happened to him and/or his sister?**

   ▶ **Would the hamster be able to return alive as happens in cartoons?**

   ▶ **Who would have suffered as a result of Sammy's actions?**

   ▶ **Does the loss of a life change the lives of others? How?**

   ▶ **Did Sammy realize that the hamster would die?**

3. ***Identify the Skill Components:*** Write the following skill components on the board, a chart or on sentence strips:

1. Consider carefully the appropriateness of the required action.

2. Consider the safety of all participants.

3. Remember that cartoons, video images, and movie situations are done with art effects.

4. Keep in mind that stunt men and special effects are used to portray danger.

5. Think about how much a person and a pet would be missed if dead.

6. Think about the good things a person and a pet can give to many.

7. Place a high value on life.

8. Respect all lives like your own.

4. ***Model the Skill:*** The teacher will act out the following scene.

A child in the class is tired of taking care of the family's tropical fish and is thinking about getting rid of them by using a drug first to kill them and then throwing the dead fish into a pond. The teacher will use a "think aloud" method to show the class how the skill components could help the child to value the life of the fish and find a way to save their lives.

5. ***Behavioral Rehearsal:***

A. *Selection:* The teacher will select students, as needed, to role play the following situations.

B. *Role Play:* (Depending on the age and role playing experience of the children, the teacher may wish to use index cards to script the role plays.)

   – A student will role play Sammy, from the introduction, using the skill components.

   – Carolyn, a sixth grader, is watching TV with her six-year-old brother, who said he liked the way Roadrunner gets smashed or blown up but is always OK the next week. She will employ the skill components in a conversation with her brother.

   – Richard wanted to "hang out" with a group of boys in his neighborhood. They said he could, but first he would have to do something bad to Mrs. Smith's cat. Mrs. Smith is very old and lives alone with only her cat for company.

   – Diedra thought she would like to join the "girls' gang" that was in her school. They told her that in order to join, she would have to participate in a drive-by shooting. Diedra will use the skill components to help her decide if this is what she really wants to do.

C. *Completion:* Following each role play, the teacher will determine if the skill components were used, and if the role play was done correctly. If yes, the role play is complete; if no, the teacher will ask the children to re-enact the role play with corrections.

D. *Reinforcers:* The teacher will praise the role players and applaud them or perhaps give them reward(s) for their participation.

E. *Discussion:* The teacher will lead a discussion about life and death. He/she could have the students share the loss of a family member or pet and how they felt to lose this person or pet. Ask students to think about and share one good thing that they might do as an adult to show why their life will have special value. (Any positive or helpful action will be accepted and applauded.)

6. **Practice:** The teacher will distribute the worksheet "Life Is Valuable" and have students complete it in class. In the lower grades, this can be done as a group activity.

7. **Independent Use:** The teacher will give the worksheet "I Will Be Valuable" to students as a take-home assignment. Students will draw a picture of themselves and state three good things they can do at their current age. Then, they will draw a picture of what they think they may look like as an adult and state three good things that they might accomplish as an adult. The teacher will encourage them to discuss their ideas with their parents.

8. **Continuation:** The teacher will take advantage of every opportunity to reinforce with the children that life is precious and so are they. They are important; and the teacher will tell them that they can become valuable adults if they always cherish life.

Name _____ Date _____

Directions: Find each of the words listed at the bottom of this page in the box below, printed horizontally or vertically. Put a line around each word when you find it.

"LIFE IS VALUABLE"

G	O	O	D	A	M	O	V	I	E	S
B	D	F	H	R	J	L	N	P	Q	R
T	U	V	W	E	X	Y	Z	A	B	C
H	I	G	H	A	D	E	F	G	P	H
I	J	V	A	L	U	A	B	L	E	K
L	S	M	N	O	S	V	W	X	T	Z
A	P	V	B	V	Z	C	A	B	D	O
S	E	E	Y	E	F	L	I	F	E	G
T	C	U	W	O	R	T	H	Y	M	Z
H	I	I	X	P	E	R	S	O	N	J
R	A	K	W	L	T	M	Q	R	N	O
Q	L	P	C	A	R	T	O	O	N	S

Life	**Good**	**Real**
Person	**Cartoons**	**Movies**
Pet	**Special**	**Live**
Valuable	**High**	**Worthy**

Name _____ Date _____

Directions: Find each of the words at the bottom of this page in the box below, printed horizontally or vertically. Put a line around each word when you find it.

"LIFE IS VALUABLE"
Answer Key

G	O	O	D	A	M	O	V	I	E	S
B	D	F	H	R	J	L	N	P	Q	R
T	U	V	W	E	X	Y	Z	A	B	C
H	I	G	H	A	D	E	F	G	P	H
I	J	V	A	L	U	A	B	L	E	K
L	S	M	N	O	S	V	W	X	T	Z
A	P	V	B	V	Z	C	A	B	D	O
S	E	E	Y	E	F	L	I	F	E	G
T	C	U	W	O	R	T	H	Y	M	Z
H	I	I	X	P	E	R	S	O	N	J
R	A	K	W	L	T	M	Q	R	N	O
Q	L	P	C	A	R	T	O	O	N	S

Life	**Good**	**Real**
Person	**Cartoons**	**Movies**
Pet	**Special**	**Live**
Valuable	**High**	**Worthy**

Name _____ Date _____

"I Will Be Valuable"

Directions:

1. Draw a picture of yourself as you are now. When you have finished drawing the picture, think of three good things you can do at your age now and write them under the picture.

2. Draw a picture of yourself as you think you will look when you are an adult. When you have finished your drawing, think of three good things you will be able to do as an adult. Write them under your picture.

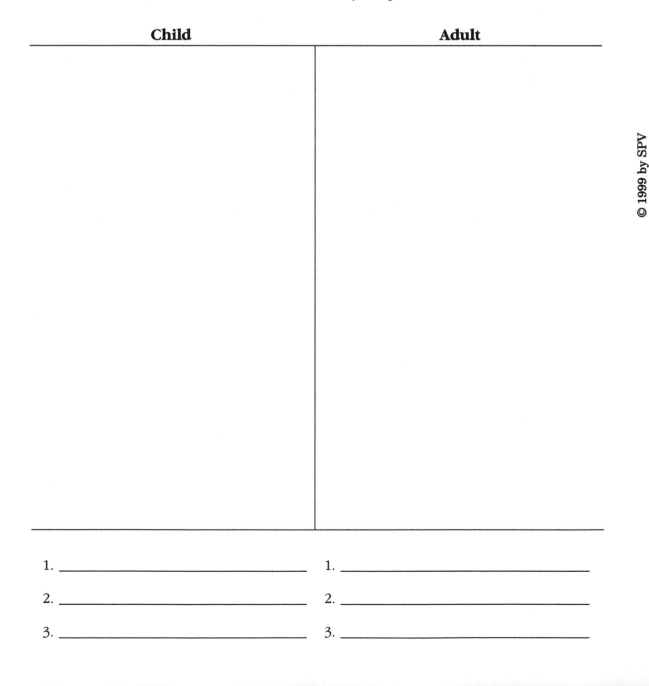

Child	**Adult**

1. _____   1. _____

2. _____   2. _____

3. _____   3. _____

Understanding How to Conquer Fear

Behavior Objective: Children will learn to separate real fear from imagined fear based on news reports of shooting, bombings, riots, and other violent events which have occurred in other locations.

Directed Lesson:

1. **Establish the Need:** Children often become fearful when they hear that something bad has occurred in school or other places located in another city or state. They fear that it might happen to them. This fear can become so real that it interferes with the students' ability to lead a normal life. Therefore, they need help to overcome the fear by understanding that precautions are taken to lessen the possibility of the same thing happening to them.

2. **Introduction:** The teacher will read the following story to the class:

   Joella was a nine-year-old who lived in a small town in the Midwest. She went to a school which had 300 children in grades K through 5. The school was located in the middle of a quiet residential area on the edge of the town. The lead story on the news last night was about a gang shooting which took place on the playground of an elementary school on the West Coast, about 2,000 miles away. The bullets from the shooting did penetrate a school window. Fortunately no one in the school was hurt.

   As Joella thought about this, she could feel herself becoming more and more fearful that this could happen at her school.

   By the time a few weeks had passed, Joella is so afraid of a gang shooting at her school that she is startled and begins to tremble at any loud "bang" type noise. Her older brother notices how jumpy she is and asks her "What's wrong?"

   The teacher will ask the following questions:

   ▶ **Why is Joella so "jumpy?"**

   ▶ **Is her fear real, imagined or both?**

   ▶ **What can be done to lessen her fear?**

3. **Identify the Skill Components:** List the skill components on the chalkboard or on a chart.

   1. Decide what is making you fearful.

   2. Consider the circumstances of the "bad happening."

   3. Think about the similarities and differences of locations.

13

4. Talk to your parent(s), teacher, counselor or principal about your fears.

5. Ask what procedures are in place for protection at locations you frequent.

6. Remember that adults will do their best to keep you safe.

4. ***Model the Skill:*** The teacher will model how to use the skill components by playing the part of Joella's brother as he asks her what is wrong. A student can assist by role playing Joella as her brother (the teacher) helps her to use the skill components to relieve her fears.

5. ***Behavioral Rehearsal:***

   A. *Selection:* The teacher will select three pairs of students to role play.

   B. *Role Play:* Each pair of students will role play one of three scenarios.

      – Sarah saw television pictures of a region being flooded due to heavy rains. Although she lives in a very dry area with little rainfall, she worries about her school or house being flooded. Sarah expresses her fear to her mother.

      – DeShawn lives in a big city. He saw pictures in the newspaper of a building that caught on fire and almost burned to the ground because the fire department was located 35 miles away and took too long to arrive due to the distance. Several children and adults were burned in the fire. DeShawn wonders if this could happen to him. DeShawn talks with a friend about this.

      – Roger heard that a boy in the other fifth grade class brought a knife to school in his bookbag and threatened to "slash" everybody who had been bothering him. The boy was removed from the class before anyone was hurt. Roger knows that he sometimes bothers other kids in his class. As he looks around the room, he notices that several kids have bookbags at their desks. His mind begins to see a knife being jabbed at him. Roger talks to the counselor.

   C. *Completion:* After each role play, the teacher and class will decide if the role play was correct. If not, the teacher will ask the children to re-enact it with corrections. If correct, the role play is complete.

   D. *Reinforcers:* The teachers and the classmates will give applause to each set of role players and will show appreciation for their efforts.

   E. *Discussion:* After the role plays, the teacher may ask the children if they have seen or heard about bad things which happened somewhere and how it made them feel. Then the teacher will discuss what can be done so that the children become less afraid of similar things happening in their close environment.

6. ***Practice:*** The teacher will have the students complete the worksheet "Planning Ahead" and share their responses in class as time permits.

7. ***Independent Use:*** The teacher will distribute the worksheet "Safety" and ask the students to complete it and return it in one week for discussion in class.

8. ***Continuation:*** The teacher will remind children that they should not go through life being afraid of everything. However, being aware of what is happening and knowing safety procedures will provide a sense of security and build confidence that they can protect themselves and handle emergency situations successfully.

Name _____ Date _____

PLANNING AHEAD

Directions: Think of a "bad thing" that could happen at school, home, or on the street and list it below. Then answer the questions about it as it relates to you.

A "bad thing" that could happen at my school or at any other location is

_____

_____

_____

1. Why does this make you feel worried or afraid?

_____

_____

_____

_____

_____

2. With whom can you discuss your thoughts and feelings about this? (List as many people as you wish.)

_____

_____

_____

_____

_____

3. How can talking with someone make you feel less worried or afraid?

_____

_____

_____

_____

_____

Name _____ Date _____

SAFETY

Directions: Describe the safety procedures used in your school for emergency situations, such as fire, a hurricane or tornado, fighting, and so on and how they help to lessen your fears, with "1" meaning no fear, "2" some fear, and "3" great fear. Next, list safety procedures established at other places listed below. If you do not know them, find out about them. List at least 2 likely emergency situations that might occur in each location. Discuss your answers with your parent(s) and ask them to help you collect the data.

Your School	**Emergency**	**Safety Procedure**	**Fear**

Swimming Pool

Mall

Playground

Home

Street

Managing Anger

Behavioral Objective: Students will learn that while everyone, at times, becomes angry, they can avoid expressing anger in a violent manner, thus avoiding verbal and physical violence and achieving a peaceful resolution.

Directed Lesson:

1. ***Establish the Need:*** Each of us becomes angry at times. It is important to learn to control our reactions when we are frustrated, embarrassed and upset by situations beyond our control and especially when they are created by others. Often simple techniques, such as placing things in perspective, allowing for a "cooling off" period and so on, will reduce the tension around us in a difficult situation and allow us to avoid a potentially-violent situation or to deal with it in a peaceful manner.

2. ***Introduction:*** The teacher will read the following story to the class:

   There was a third-grade class at Hopwood School. It was a class that had a very nice young teacher named Ms. Stewart. She was always pleasant and had a real "love" for her students. Among her twenty-four students were two boys, Raymon and Bobby. They were often, as boys are, tough and quick. Bobby was also a boy who sometimes did not share things well with others. Ms. Stewart gave the class an assignment to draw their impressions of a recent field trip or visit that they had taken to the local fair.

   She provided a box of coloring crayons at each of the work tables where students were assigned to work in groups of four. Soon after they started their work, both boys wanted to use the yellow crayon. Bobby yelled to Raymon, "Give me that crayon." Raymon said "Wait!" Bobby then grabbed for it and Raymon pulled it away and made a bad comment under his breath. Bobby got up and moved rapidly around the table to come after Raymon. Ms. Stewart quickly moved to the table to come between the two boys who were now standing face to face. Bobby swung his fist and Ms. Stewart was hit, with her glasses flying off her face. . . .

   The teacher will ask the following questions:

   ▶ **Could this incident have been avoided?**

   ▶ **How?**

   ▶ **What should each boy have done?**

   ▶ **Do you think Bobby meant to hit Ms. Stewart?**

   ▶ **How could Bobby have handled this situation in a non-violent manner?**

17

3. ***Identify the Skill Components:*** Write the following skill components on the board or on sentence strips:

1. Think about what you are feeling.

2. Decide why you are really angry.

3. Give yourself time to *think first.*

4. Consider how you can maintain control.

5. Decide how to handle the situation.

6. Find a peaceful resolution.

4. ***Model the Skill:*** The teacher will role play Bobby from the story in the introduction and use the skill components in a "think aloud" fashion to show how Bobby could have handled the situation and his anger in a peaceful manner.

5. ***Behavioral Rehearsal:***

   A. *Selection:* The teacher will students to role play the following situations in pairs of two.

   B. *Role Play:* The teacher will ask each pair of students to do one of the following five role plays.
   - Your mother was called a name by another student at school.
   - You received a poor grade on your report card.
   - A student pushed in front of you in the lunch line.
   - A group of two students laughed at your worn pants with other students nearby.
   - A student taped a sign on the back of your shirt that read "I'm a sucker."

   C. *Completion:* After each role play, the teacher and class will discuss how well the skill components were used in the role plays. If corrections are necessary, the teacher will ask the students to re-enact the role play. If there are none, the role play is complete.

   D. *Reinforcers:* All participants in the role plays will be recognized and given praise.

   E. *Discussion:* The teacher will start the discussion by asking the following questions:
   - **What emotions were evident in each of the role plays? (answers to be noted on the board)**
   - **Why do we seem to get angry in upsetting situations?**
   - **Why is it important that we seek non-violent and non-physical solutions to upsetting situations?**

6. ***Practice:*** The teacher will distribute clean sheets of paper and have the students draw facial expressions of persons with emotions (or feelings) as described in the Discussion section (5E) of the lesson and noted on the board. They will then describe the emotions they intended to show in their drawings and discuss these with the class.

7. ***Independent Use:*** The teacher will distribute the worksheet entitled: "Angry Situations" and ask the students to return it after one week for discussion.

8. ***Continuation:*** Periodically, the class teacher will bring in an article from the newspaper which describes a violent situation which occurred and use it to reinforce the importance of learning how to manage anger by promoting a brief classroom discussion.

Name _____   Date _____

ANGRY SITUATIONS

Directions: For the next five days, observe family members, friends, and classmates for situations that cause anger. Write a sentence describing each "angry situation" that you observe. You may draw a picture to accompany your writing.

Angry Situation #1

_____

_____

_____

Angry Situation #2

_____

_____

_____

Angry Situation #3

_____

_____

_____

Angry Situation #4

_____

_____

_____

Angry Situation #5

_____

_____

_____

Learning That Retaliation Is Futile

Behavioral Objective: Students will learn that retaliating for something done wrong to them "just for the spite of it," is unproductive and does not make anyone feel good. On the contrary, it can lead to bad and serious consequences, such as tears, fights, and violence.

Directed Lesson:

1. ***Establish the Need:*** Children, just as some adults, feel that if they have been "wronged" even unintentionally, they have to do the same in return—namely, retaliate. Retaliation frequently starts fights which can become nasty and violent. Therefore, children have to learn the futility and consequences of "giving back" more of the same than was done to them. They also will have to understand that some "wrong doing" is done without bad intent and should be accepted, especially after an apology.

2. ***Introduction:*** The teacher will read the following story:

   Sara and Rachel were playing with Sara's most loved puzzle. Rachel accidentally lost some pieces and they started arguing about it. Rachel apologized, and told Sara that she had misplaced those pieces and just could not find them, but Sara was angry and just decided to go home and left without her game. Sara's mother said it was not necessary for Rachel to replace the game because Sara should not have taken it out of her own house anyway. Sara was very unhappy at having lost this game and was getting very upset with Rachel.

   A few weeks later a big commotion started at school when Rachel was missing one of her favorite games. It turned up broken in the trash can. Jane said she saw Sara throw it in the trash can. When Rachel heard this, she pledged never again to play with Sara.

   The teacher will ask the following questions:

   ▶ **Do you believe that Jane told the truth?**

   ▶ **Do you think Sara did destroy Rachel's game?**

   ▶ **Why did Sara throw out Rachel's game?**

   ▶ **Was it retaliation?**

   ▶ **How did Sara feel after getting caught?**

   ▶ **Should Sara have thrown out Rachel's game, even if Rachel had thrown away the missing puzzle pieces?**

3. ***Identify the Skill Components:*** Write the following skill components on the board or on sentence strips.

20

1. Consider your reasons for wanting to retaliate.
2. Analyze what retaliation can do for you.
3. Study your feelings.
4. Weigh benefits and futilities.
5. Think of all possible consequences.
6. Find alternative solutions (forgiveness, discussion).
7. Act accordingly.

4. ***Model the Skill:*** The teacher will role play a student who wants to retaliate against a class-mate who spilled milk over her/his favorite pants in the lunchroom. The teacher will select a student to portray the child that spilled the milk. By using the skill components, the teacher will show the children how to arrive at a more satisfactory solution than doing something to get even.

5. ***Behavioral Rehearsal:***

   A. *Selection:* The teacher will select three groups of an appropriate number of children.

   B. *Role Play:* Each group will role play one of the following scenarios:
      - A group of three will role play the story from the Introduction.
      - One child causes another to trip and fall.
      - One child borrows a bicycle and returns it with a broken handle bar.

   C. *Completion:* After each role play, the teacher will decide if the role play was done correctly and if the skill components were used appropriately. If corrections are needed, the role plays will be re-enacted; if not, the role play is complete.

   D. *Reinforcers:* The teacher and class will thank the role players for their participation with applause and verbal compliments.

   E. *Discussion:* The teacher will start the discussion by asking the following questions:
      ❱ **Why is retaliation a futile act?**
      ❱ **Can retaliation lead to serious consequences? How?**
      ❱ **What are some better solutions than retaliating?**
      ❱ **Is forgiving a virtue?**

6. ***Practice:*** The teacher will distribute the worksheet "Retaliation: to complete and share in class.

7. ***Independent Use:*** The teacher will distribute the worksheet "Get Even" for the children to take home and return completed in one week for discussion in class.

8. ***Continuation:*** The teacher will indicate that during our entire life, situations will occur which make us sufficiently angry to create feelings of revenge. Since revenge is futile, children and adults should forget retaliation and rather forgive and discuss how to prevent similar situations in the future.

Name _____ Date _____

Retaliation

Directions: Use the words in the balloon below to complete the following sentences.

retaliation
discuss
get even
hurt
feel
fight
responsible
forgive
non-violent
talk

1. What is a reason why you want _____ ?

2. A _____ way of working out a problem is best.

3. It is okay to _____ hurt if someone wrongs us.

4. To _____ does not settle the situation.

5. It is better to _____ it out.

6. It is better to _____ than to _____ .

7. It is better to _____ than to _____ .

Directions: Write down the skill components.

1. _____

2. _____

3. _____

4. _____

5. _____

6. _____

7. _____

Name _____ Date _____

Retaliation
Answer Key

Directions: Use the words in the balloon below to complete the following sentences.

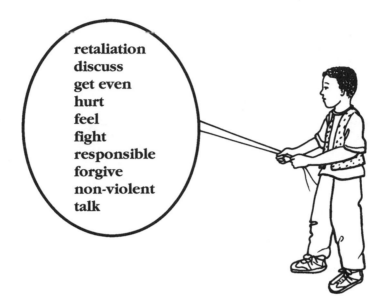

retaliation
discuss
get even
hurt
feel
fight
responsible
forgive
non-violent
talk

1. What is a reason why you want ___retaliation?___

2. A ___responsible___ way of working out a problem is best.

3. It is okay to ___feel___ hurt if someone wrongs us.

4. To ___get even___ does not settle the situation.

5. It is better to ___talk___ it out.

6. It is better to ___forgive___ than to ___hurt___ .

7. It is better to ___discuss___ than to fight .

Name _____ Date _____

GET EVEN

Directions: Describe a situation at home or in school where you felt the need to retaliate. Describe what you did. If you had to do it over, how would you handle the same situation now? Describe whether the skill components are helpful and how you used them. Discuss this assignment with your parents.

_____

_____

_____

_____

_____

_____

_____

_____

_____

Draw two pictures

HOW I REACTED THEN   HOW I WOULD REACT NOW

Learning to Care for the Handicapped

Behavioral Objective: Students will learn that people with handicaps need, like themselves, care, help and attention and should be treated as equals and with courtesy.

Directed Lesson:

1. **Establish the Need:** Children are frequently cruel and often ridicule people who are handicapped and cannot function the same as they do. They must learn that the handicapped person yearns to be accepted and treated as an equal and that cruelty might end up in injury.

2. **Introduction:** The teacher will read the following story:

> Due to an injury Johnny received while riding his bicycle, his left arm became paralyzed and would remain that way for the rest of his life. The accident occurred while Johnny was in elementary school. He learned from the beginning that because of his permanently injured arm, he was handicapped and different than his classmates and friends who were able to use both arms.
>
> Johnny also learned quickly that not all people are understanding of a person who is different due to a handicap. Some of the kids would call him cruel names, such as "one-arm" or "Captain Hook!"
>
> He would watch as the other kids played sports, like football, basketball and baseball. Johnny and his father would go to all of the _____ _____ baseball games. Johnny told his father that baseball was his favorite sport and that he especially wanted to play it, but that he also thought he would never get a chance to be a baseball player.
>
> Johnny remembered the time when he begged the other kids to let him play. Since they were short one person, Billy told him he could be the catcher. Billy, being the pitcher, thought to show Johnny off and threw a very hard ball at Johnny, so that when Johnny tried to catch the ball, it knocked him to the ground. Almost all of the kids were now laughing at Johnny as he began to cry. Finally, Jeff came over and helped Johnny get up off the ground.

The teacher will ask students the following questions:

- **How do you think Johnny was feeling.**
- **How do you think Billy was feeling?**
- **Is there anything that anyone could have done to change the situation that led to this?**
- **What is a handicap? Was Johnny handicapped? (A student might be asked to find a definition of handicap in the dictionary, or the teacher can give a definition.)**
- **What can be done to show respect towards people with handicaps?**

3. ***Identify the Skill Components:*** Write the skill components on the board or on sentence strips.

   1. Realize that there are many people with handicaps.

   2. Consider their special needs.

   3. Understand that people with handicaps should be treated as equals and with courtesy.

   4. Learn to make them feel welcomed.

   5. Realize that they can be your most valuable friends.

   6. Be their friend.

4. ***Model the Skill:*** The teacher will model the skill by making use of the skill components in the following situation: A new student joins the class. He looks very normal, but when he speaks he has a problem with lisping and sometimes with stuttering when getting excited or nervous. The teacher will portray a classmate of the new student and will ask one child in the class to role play the new student.

5. ***Behavioral Rehearsal:***

   A. *Selection:* The teacher will select two groups of four students to role play the story about Johnny.

   B. *Role Play:* The students will role play Johnny, his father, Billy and Jeff in the Introduction using the skill components.

   C. *Completion:* Following the role play, the teacher will reinforce correct behaviors, identify inappropriate behaviors, and ask the students to re-enact role play with corrections, if needed. If there are no corrections, role play is complete.

   D. *Reinforcers:* Compliments and applause from the teacher and students will acknowledge the efforts of the role players.

   E. *Discussion:* The teacher will use the following questions to encourage discussion about the skill:

   ▶ **Why do some students ridicule and act cruel to people with a handicap?**

   ▶ **How should you treat handicaps?**

   ▶ **Why do you think we should help someone with a handicap?**

   ▶ **What are some types of handicaps?**

6. ***Practice:*** Distribute copies of the worksheet entitled "Care" for students to complete and to discuss in class.

7. ***Independent Use:*** Hand out copies of the log sheet "Look Out," which students will use to record observations of people with handicaps. With the help of parents or guardians, students can make their observations around the school, at home, in church, in their neighborhood, or any other public place. After two weeks, they should return their completed log sheets and share them with the class.

8. ***Continuation:*** The teacher will remind students that throughout their lives, they will come in contact with people with handicaps. By being tolerant towards handicapped persons and caring, the students will realize that they will gain much satisfaction, increased self-esteem, insight, and enjoyment.

Name _____ Date _____

CARE

Directions: Under each handicap listed below, write down some acts or things you might do to show that you care for this person.

HANDICAP #1   **Person is confined to a wheelchair**

_____

_____

_____

_____

_____

_____

HANDICAP #2   **Person is blind**

_____

_____

_____

_____

_____

_____

HANDICAP #3   **Person is really overweight**

_____

_____

_____

_____

_____

_____

Name _____ Date _____

LOOK OUT

Directions: Complete the log sheet. (Use the skill components.)

LOG SHEET

Person with Handicap	Where Observed	People's Reaction to This Person	What Did You Do

Learning That Failures Can Lead to Success

Behavioral Objective: Children will learn that failures are not "all bad" since failures present opportunities for improvement and that accepting failures, in good spirit, will improve their chances of future success.

Directed Lesson:

1. **Establish the Need:** Children, just like adults, frequently respond to failures by being ornery and unruly and sometimes even violent due to their feeling of having been unable to master the task they were convinced they could accomplish. Children must understand that failures followed by repeat performance will help to accomplish assured success. Therefore, it is best to accept failures by being "a good sport" and on good behavior and use failures as a step towards success.

2. **Introduction:** The teacher will present the following story:

   Latonia was excited about being chosen by her gym teacher to run track at the district school meet on Saturday. She was the fastest girl in her third grade class and enjoyed running and jumping over the hurdles. Everyone in the school, it seemed, came up to her and wished her well in representing the school.

   Friday night Latonia was so excited she could hardly sleep. When it became her turn to run in the race on Saturday, she was nervous, but was confident that she would win. The race was close, but Latonia lost.

   Latonia did not say a word and ran to the locker room. She was so angry that she kicked the lockers and knocked over wastebaskets. She pushed a classmate aside who tried to talk with her. The next day in school, she cut class and stayed in the lavatory for hours until a teacher found her and sent her home. How did Latonia behave? Why?

3. **Identify the Skill Components:** Write the following skill components on the board or on sentence strips.

   1. Determine why you failed.

   2. Consider failure to be an experience.

   3. Accept failure in good spirit.

   4. Use failure as an experience.

   5. Learn from your failure.

   6. Look forward to success.

4. ***Model the Skill Components:*** The teacher will role play Latonia in the story of the Introduction and show the class, using a thought process, how Latonia would have acted by using the skill components.

5. ***Behavioral Rehearsal:***

   A. *Selection:* The teacher will select three pairs of students to perform role plays.

   B. *Role Play:* Each pair of children will play one of the three following scenarios:

      – Mary and Louise play ping pong and Mary wins all the time.

      – Peter and Jacob have a bet about who is winning in a running race of about 10 minutes, around the block. Peter loses by 10 seconds.

      – Bill and Patty are in a spelling contest. Patty wins.

   C. *Completion:* After each role play, reinforce correct behavior, identify inappropriate behaviors and re-enact role play with corrections. If there are no corrections, role play is complete.

   D. *Reinforcers:* The teacher will give praise to the students for their performances and the class will applaud them profusely.

   E. *Discussion:* The teacher will start a discussion by asking the following questions:

      ▶ **How do you think Latonia felt when she did not win the race?**

      ▶ **What do you think will be the consequences for her response to failure?**

      ▶ **Explain why Latonia responded in the way she did.**

      ▶ **Using the skill components, how would you respond?**

6. ***Practice:*** The teacher will distribute the worksheet "Better Days Ahead" to complete in class and discuss.

7. ***Independent Use:*** The teacher will give the children the worksheet "Slipping and Tripping" to take home and return completed in one week for discussion in class.

8. ***Continuation:*** The teacher will stress whenever an opportunity presents itself that failures should be accepted in good spirit and used as a step to success and that responding to failures with unruly and violent behaviors will make situations worse and not better.

Name _____ Date _____

BETTER DAYS AHEAD

Directions:

1. Write about a time you failed to do as well as you expected at something.

_____

_____

_____

_____

_____

_____

_____

2. How did you respond to that failure?

_____

_____

_____

_____

_____

_____

_____

3. If you had to do it over how would you respond now? Use the skill components to respond more appropriately.

_____

_____

_____

_____

_____

_____

_____

Name _____   Date _____

SLIPPING AND TRIPPING

Directions: Talk with your parent(s) about a time in their youth when they failed at something, if possible when they were your age. Write their experience down.

_____

_____

_____

_____

_____

- Ask your parent(s) if they learned something from their failure and write down what they tell you.

_____

_____

_____

- Write down the skill components first, and then explain how you can use the skill components in a similar situation.

_____

_____

_____

_____

_____

_____   _____
Parent's Signature   Date

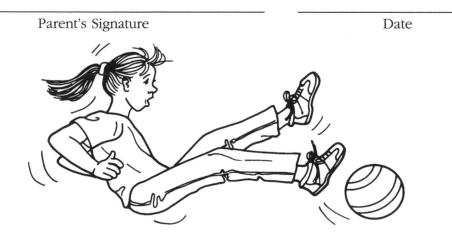

Learning to React to Disrespect

Behavioral Objective: Youngsters will learn what disrespect is, why disrespect hurts one's feelings, and how to react in a constructive, non-violent way and keep dignity.

Directed Lesson:

1. ***Establish the Need:*** At times, students use disrespectful remarks, gestures and acts toward their classmates, teachers, parents and others which can lead to verbal rebuttals and even fights. Disrespectful remarks, gestures, and acts are frequently made on purpose in order to rile other persons and get a reaction from them. Serious problems can occur when the reaction results in aggression and violence between the parties. Students need to recognize when a disrespectful remark, gesture, and act is being made only for the purpose of getting a violent reaction. In this case, they will learn either to ignore it or to respond in a non-combative manner. Even if the disrespect is part of an angry outburst, they will learn to handle it in a way that prevents escalation to more serious violence. In essence, students will learn to "keep their cool" in the face of disrespect.

2. ***Introduction:*** The teacher will read the following story:

   Billy, who is bigger than the other fifth-grade boys, is standing with a group of boys outside the school, when he sees Eugene walking toward them. Billy says to the other boys, "Watch this!" When Eugene is just about face to face with the group, Billy steps out in front of Eugene and says sarcastically, "Hey, U-Gene, did your mother pick out those clothes you're wearing?" Eugene is tired of being "dissed" because of his name. The kids think it's a sissy name and show him little respect. He has had enough and is ready to give back what he has been getting. So, he clenches his fists and opens his mouth to speak.

   The teacher will ask the children the following questions:

   ▶ **How did Billy show disrespect to Eugene?**
   ▶ **What do you think Billy wanted to happen?**
   ▶ **What do you think Eugene will say or do?**
   ▶ **What could happen as a result of what Eugene says and does?**
   ▶ **Is there anything that Eugene could do to handle his reaction to this kind of disrespect that would prevent the use of verbal or physical violence?**

3. ***Skill Components:*** Write the skill components on a chart or on the chalkboard.

   1. Consider how you are being treated.

   2. Determine whether disrespect was intended.

   3. If not, forget about it.

   4. If yes, think about why the other person disrespects you.

    5. Remember, that respect for yourself is most important.

    6. Think of possible consequences due to your response.

    7. Take your time before you react.

    8. Decide a careful response.

4. ***Model the Skill:*** The teacher will model the use of the skill components for the following situation: On Monday morning, fourth grader Tyler greets the teacher by saying, "Hey, dude!" Tyler has been warned before not to use this greeting with the teacher.

5. ***Behavioral Rehearsal:***

    A. *Selection:* The teacher will select three groups of students for the role plays.

    B. *Role Plays:* The teacher will ask each group of children to role play one of the following scenarios:

        – Freddie stutters when he becomes nervous. As Freddie begins his oral book report, the stuttering also begins. Beth starts to imitate Freddie to the delight of the rest of the class.

        – Jacob wore his new shirt and pants to school because after school his parents were taking him to see his grandmother at the nursing home to celebrate her 89th birthday. The other boys called him "Granny's boy" when he refused to play football at recess.

        – Mary is a slow learner in a third grade classroom. She tries hard, but often makes mistakes when answering the teacher's questions. Today, on the playground, Joanne, again, calls her a "retard."

    C. *Completion:* After each role play, the teacher and class will reinforce the correct behaviors, identify inappropriate behaviors, and the teacher will ask the children to re-enact the role play with corrections, if necessary. If there are no corrections, the role play is complete.

    D. *Reinforcers:* The teacher and class will applaud the role players. The teacher may use other rewards as he/she deems appropriate.

    E. *Discussion:* The teacher will ask the students how to distinguish between unintended and willful disrespect. The teacher will ask the children to describe examples of disrespect that they have experienced and how the skill components could have helped them to react.

6. ***Practice:*** The teacher will hand out the worksheet "Disrespect vs. Respect" and ask children to complete the worksheet and share their answers.

7. ***Independent Use:*** The teacher will distribute copies of the worksheet "Respect in the Family" for children to complete at home and bring back to class in one week. At that time, children can share their ideas for eliminating disrespect in the family.

8. ***Continuation:*** The teacher will explain to the children that some situations, in school as well as life in general, may seem to be disrespectful, when disrespect was not intentional; at other times they will have to deal with persons who are actually disrespectful. Therefore, it will be of great benefit to children now and when they become adults to be able to think carefully how to differentiate between actual and perceived disrespect and how to react to each in a way that will not result in violence or harm to themselves or others.

Name _____   Date _____

Disrespect Vs. Respect

Directions: Read each statement. Put a line through the disrespectful statements and draw a smiley face ☺ in front of the respectful statements.

1. Hi, Sally. You look nice today.

2. Jason is a Mason jar, ha-ha-ha.

3. Wow, what a junky car your father drives!

4. Tyrone, your pitching was great!

5. You couldn't hit the side of a barn.

6. I really liked the way you cleaned your room!

7. Do your glasses help you to see better?

8. Who are you looking at, dummy?

9. Get out of my way!

10. You are my best friend.

Name _____   Date _____

Directions: Talk with your parents and other children in your family to decide how to make sure that disrespect does not cause problems for your family. Use the statements on the house to help you decide how to promote respect in your family.

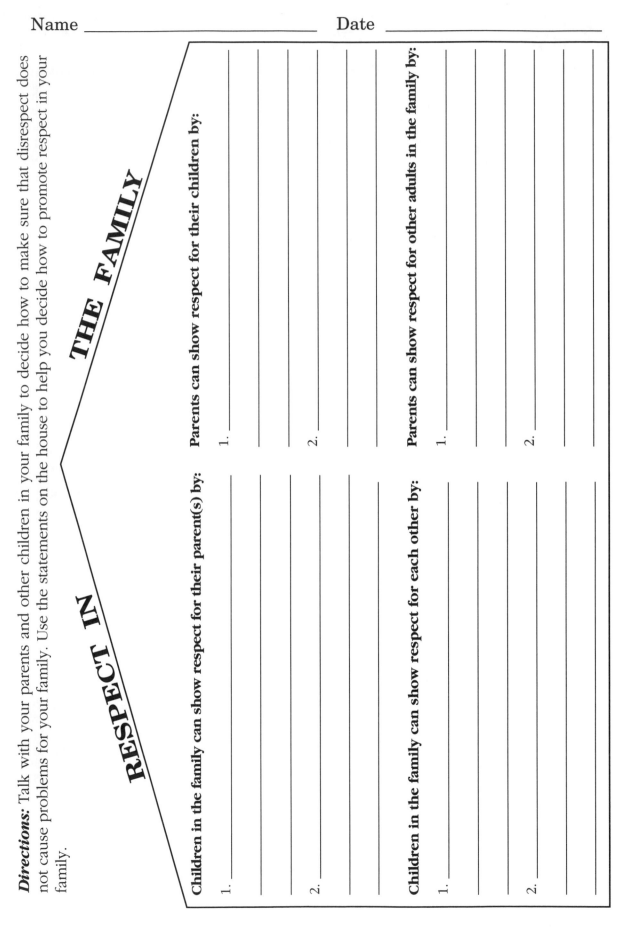

RESPECT IN THE FAMILY

Parents can show respect for their children by:

1. _____

2. _____

Parents can show respect for other adults in the family by:

1. _____

2. _____

Children in the family can show respect for their parent(s) by:

1. _____

2. _____

Children in the family can show respect for each other by:

1. _____

2. _____

Selecting Trusted Role Models

Behavioral Objective: Students will learn the importance of evaluating the behavior of potential role models by observing their lifestyles and their relation to others to decide if they lead a clean, respectful, healthy and productive life. They will, as a result, be able to select appropriate role models whom they can trust and guide them in life.

Directed Lesson:

1. **Establish the Need:** Often, young people look for inspiration and guidance to persons who they have known for a long time and who are either family members or close friends. At times, these persons might have acquired a questionable lifestyle, which propels them to encourage the young to become involved in anti-social or socially-unacceptable behavior/activities which have a negative impact on their future. The students will learn that it is extremely important to be very careful and to be discerning in the selection of a person they can trust and consider to be their role model.

2. **Introduction:** The teacher will read the following story to the class:

   The fifth grade class at Thomas Jefferson Elementary School was very lucky because their teacher was Mrs. Miller. She was the kind of teacher that did everything for her students.

   Mrs. Miller treated everyone as equals and never showed any bias or dislikes. She treated every student as if he or she were her own son or daughter and always showed respect for them.

   Even when students had problems away from school, Mrs. Miller was there for them. When Robin John's house had a bad fire, she helped raise money and clothing for her family. Another student was hit by a car and Mrs. Miller visited that student every day in the hospital.

   Whenever a student had a problem or needed someone to talk to, Mrs. Miller was always there for him/her. She was a person whom everyone trusted because they felt Mrs. Miller really cared about them.

   The teacher will begin by asking class members the following questions and will list the answers on the board:

   ▶ **Was Mrs. Miller a good role model? Why?**

   ▶ **What are some positive characteristics you recognize in a "good" person?**

   ▶ **Who are some people who could be a good role model for you? Why?**

   ▶ **What characteristics do they have?**

> How can your friends and adults, especially a role model, influence you as a young person?

> Are adults also influenced by role models?

The teacher, then, will review the life of a famous person in history, such as Mahatma Ghandi, Martin Luther King, or George Washington.

The class will then be asked to identify the characteristics these person(s) possess, such as

- Moral
- Health
- Personal
- Others
- Social

The students will then discuss characteristics which they believe are important to developing strong friendships and to choosing role models of appropriate stature.

3. ***Identify the Skill Components:*** Write the following skill components on the board or on sentence strips:

1. Think of the characteristics you want for a person you trust to be your role model.

2. Study this person's everyday behavior and lifestyle.

3. Decide if this person's behaviors are acceptable for you to imitate.

4. Consider if this person is trustworthy.

5. Realize that you need to take responsibility for your actions.

6. Show confidence in your role model's advice.

4. ***Model the Skill:*** The teacher will tell of a person who was his/her role model in life when he/she was the same age as the students in the class. Based on the situation described, the teacher will tell how the skill components could be used in reaching a decision about whom to select as a "true friend" and a "role model."

5. ***Behavioral Rehearsal:***

A. *Selection:* The teacher will select three students, each of whom will select another student in class to serve as their role model.

B. *Role Play:* Each of the three selected students will role play by telling why they selected this other student to be his/her role model and list the key reasons (personal traits) on the board. The students will be asked by the teacher to use the skill components.

To make it more interesting, the teacher will ask each of the three students to have one of the following reasons for needing a role model:

- Drug addiction.
- Fascinated by guns.
- Poor learner.

C. *Completion:* After each role play, the teacher will reinforce correct behavior and ask the students to re-enact role play with corrected behavior. The role play is complete when it is done correctly.

D. *Reinforcers:* Both the teacher and class will offer applause and praise for those students participating in the role plays.

E. *Discussion:* The class, with the teacher's leadership, will review how the skill components can be effectively used to arrive at the selection of a role model.

6. ***Practice:*** Divide the class into as many groups of three students each as the class size will allow. Then distribute to each group copies of the worksheet "Role Model" to complete and discuss in class.

7. ***Independent Use:*** The teacher will fold in half sufficient numbers of 8-1/2 x 11" sheets of heavy paper or cardboard to provide one for every member of the class. The teacher will then distribute one folded sheet to each student to take home with instructions for creating a greeting card like that shown on the following page entitled "Greeting Card."

The greeting card should be entitled "Be My Role Model" on the front and include artwork below which they deem appropriate and a message inside that explains why the child has selected this person as his/her role model. The student should sign his/her name after the message.

Ask the students to return their finished greeting cards within the week to share with the class.

8. ***Continuation:*** The teacher will periodically reinforce the importance of selecting positive role models. He/she will also frequently clip relevant news articles about positive role models in the community and use these for follow-up class discussions.

Name _____ Date _____

ROLE MODEL

Directions: Draw a caricature of a role model selected from history, friends, family or school, and describe the reasons for making the selection.

GREETING CARD

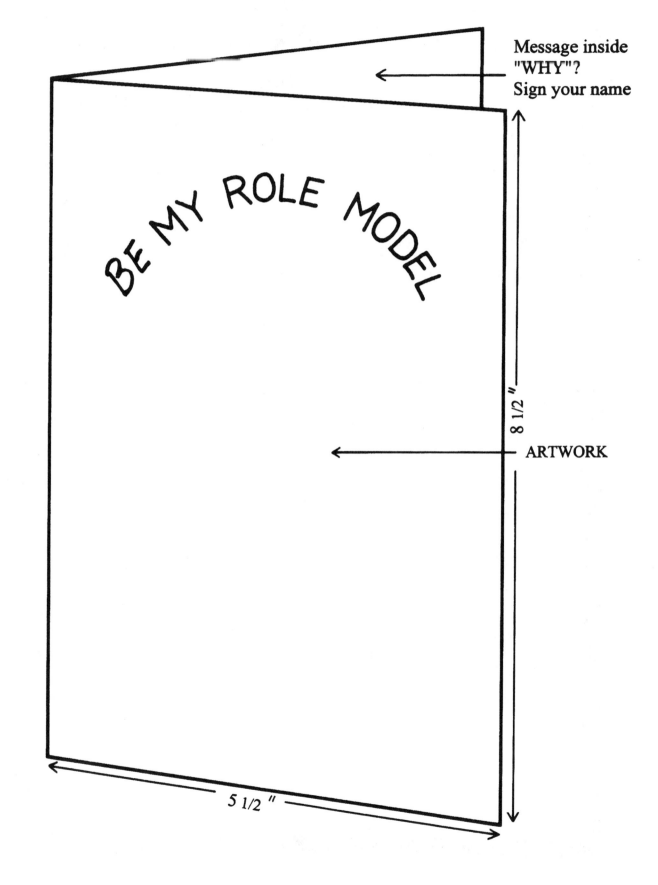

Message inside
"WHY"?
Sign your name

BE MY ROLE MODEL

8 1/2 "

ARTWORK

5 1/2 "

Leaning to Find Acceptance Without Coercion

Behavioral Objective: Students will learn that being accepted and being welcomed by others can be achieved without threats and/or bribes when good communication skills are used.

Directed Lessons:

1. **Establish the Need:** Students frequently have difficulties being accepted into circles of intimate and long-time friendships. This is especially the case when a third child seeks the friendship with two children who have been very close friends for many years. Students have to learn that to be accepted they have to establish good understanding with others by employing carefully-planned communication skills and that they should never use threats or bribes for gaining friendships.

2. **Introduction:** The teacher will read the following story to the class:

   Jennifer and Tracy had been friends for several years. They would walk to school together and sleep over at one another's house. It was nice to have someone living nearby to have fun with. There were other girls they would play with at times, but it was always Jennifer and Tracy who were close with each other.

   One day Nancy called Jennifer at home to offer her some favors to become her friend. Jennifer accepted the favors. Then Nancy started to sit with Jennifer and Tracy at lunch. Tracy felt that Nancy was intruding, but she did not say anything to Jennifer. As a matter of fact, Tracy was very quiet.

   Then one day when all three girls were leaving the lunchroom, Nancy accidentally picked up Tracy's spelling book. Tracy immediately pushed Nancy, grabbed the spelling book, and yelled "You're trying to steal my book!"

   Nancy and Jennifer looked wide-eyed at Tracy and asked "What is the matter with you?" Tracy just took her book and stormed off. Tracy was angry and knew that she had made a scene, but she felt that everything that used to be fine between Jennifer and her was gone. Nancy had had to butt in and destroy their friendship. Why?

   It was hard for Tracy to accept Nancy, and she did not know how to handle it.

   The teacher will ask the following questions:

   - **How did Tracy communicate her dislike for Nancy?**
   - **What was the real problem?**
   - **How would you have responded if you were Tracy?**
   - **How could Tracy learn better ways of communicating?**

> ❯ **What could Nancy do to ease the relationship?**
> ❯ **Did Nancy communicate well?**
> ❯ **Was it right for Nancy to use bribes with Jennifer?**

3. ***Identify the Skill Components:*** List the following skill components on the board or write them on sentence strips before class.

   1. Assess your need for relationships.

   2. Assess everybody's contribution to a relationship.

   3. Avoid showing preferences.

   4. Learn to know the weak and strong traits of all members of the group you want to join.

   5. Discuss the activities they and you like.

   6. Communicate in a careful and understanding way.

   7. Create good feelings.

   8. Communicate interest.

   9. Act friendly.

4. ***Model the Skill:*** The teacher will role play someone who is looking for friends, having just moved into town and started in a new school. The teacher will ask a child to role play the person he/she wants to befriend and demonstrate how the skill components can be used to decide how to communicate to find acceptance.

5. ***Behavioral Rehearsal:***

   A. *Selection:* The teacher will select one group of three children and two groups of two children.

   B. *Role Play:* The teacher will ask each of the groups to role play the following scenario:

      – The group of three will role play Nancy, Tracy and Jennifer from the story in the Introduction.

      – One group of two will role play a student on the playground who seeks to be accepted by a team leader to join in the game of the classmates.

      – The other group of two will role play two step-children. One stepchild just joined the family of his/her mother with a stepfather and his child. The two children will use the skill components to learn to accept each other's friendship.

   C. *Completion:* After each role play, the teacher will reinforce correct behavior, identify inappropriate behaviors and re-enact role play with corrections. If there are no corrections, role play is complete.

   D. *Reinforcers:* The teacher will thank the students for role playing and ask the class to join in congratulating the classmates for their well-done performances.

   E. *Discussion:* The teacher will start a discussion by asking the following questions:

      > ❯ **How do you establish friendships?**
      > ❯ **Why is it better to use communication skills than threats or bribes?**
      > ❯ **Can bribes lead to violence?**

43

▶ **Whose attitude was wrong in the story about Jennifer and Tracy?**

▶ **Is it best to communicate with all concerned in the friendship? Why?**

6. ***Practice:*** The teacher will distribute copies of the worksheet "Accepted" and ask the students to complete it and discuss their answers in class.

7. ***Independent Use:*** The teacher will distribute copies of the worksheet "Friends" to complete at home and return in one week for discussion in class.

8. ***Continuation:*** The teacher will point out that persons who understand to make themselves wanted as friends will be rich in experience throughout their entire lives. The teacher will emphasize that students shall always use communication skills rather than threats and bribes to find acceptance by others.

Name _____   Date _____

Accepted

Directions: Tell in a complete sentence if you would most likely accept a child to be a friend if he/she is similar to you. If you would, write your answer to the question in each balloon. If you would rather have a friend with different traits, talk about yourself in the left half of the balloon and about the friend you seek or would accept in the right side of the same balloon after you connect the vertical center lines in each balloon.

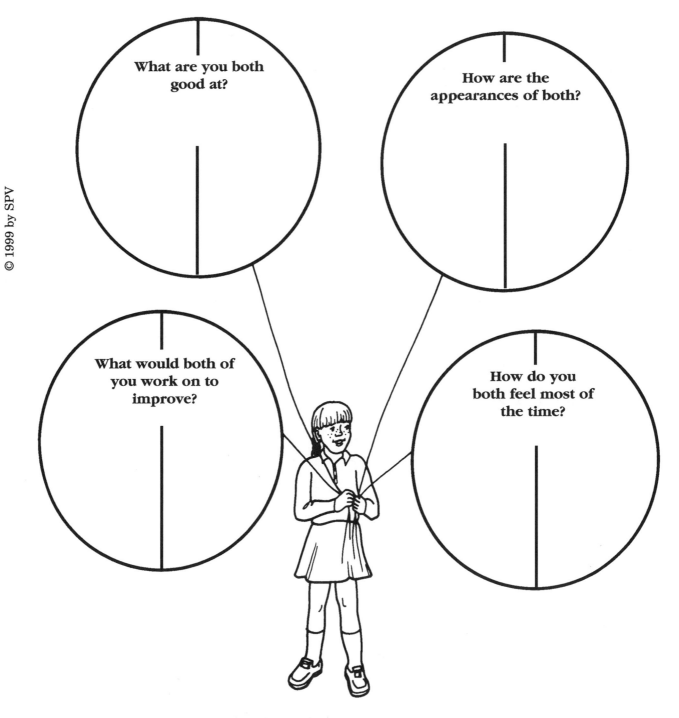

What are you both good at?

How are the appearances of both?

What would both of you work on to improve?

How do you both feel most of the time?

Name _____ Date _____

Friends

Directions: In one paragraph or more, describe how you would communicate with someone to find acceptance—to become a friend of him or her and his/her friends. (Use the skill components.) Then answer the following questions and discuss your answers with your parents.

_____

_____

_____

_____

_____

_____

How do you start a conversation?

_____

_____

What do you look for in friends?

_____

_____

How do you treat a friend?

_____

_____

How do you keep a friend?

_____

_____

Why is it important to have friends?

_____

_____

Should you ever use threats or bribes to gain friendship? _____

Developing Good Friendships

Behavioral Objective: Students will learn that friendships need time to develop and that friends do not have to be alike. Close and good friendships can be formed by individuals with very diverse attributes and coming from different cultures.

Directed Lesson:

1. **Establish the Need:** Young people frequently look for friends who are like themselves and who enjoy all the same activities, expressions and emotions. In many instances, fights and ridicule develop between youngsters because they do not want to tolerate and accept any likes and dislikes that are different from their own. Their first impulse is often to start fights to negate brutally any acceptance of different behavior and taste. Therefore, they have to learn to understand that strong bonds and most extraordinary friendships can be developed between very diverse people if they give the relationship time to grow.

2. **Introduction:** The teacher will read the following story to the class:

   Sheila was a very outgoing and aggressive type of girl. She wasn't afraid to say or do anything. Sheila had lots of friends and was always reaching out to excel. Her parents had money to spend on her wishes, and she was spoiled. Lisa, on the other hand, was a very quiet and shy girl. She didn't have a lot of friends, mainly because she was so shy, but also because her parents could not afford extras for her. When it came to being smart and getting good grades, Lisa was the top student in her class.

   One day the teacher, Miss Wilson, told the class that she was going to pair students for an assignment that was to be researched on the Internet. The teacher paired Sheila with Lisa. When they started working together in the library, it seemed that this pairing was not going to work. Sheila tried to be friendly in her aggressive way, but Lisa, who seemed somewhat intimidated by Sheila and her spending habits and maybe also jealous and defensive, remained shy, passive and simply quiet.

   At first, it seemed that the two girls might get into a real fight, but as days passed and the two continued working together on their assignment, things began to happen. Lisa, who was quiet in the beginning now started talking more. She even became somewhat outgoing. She told Sheila that deep down inside, she always wanted to be just like her and to have lots of friends and spending money. Sheila told Lisa that she always wanted to be as smart as she was and to excel by getting those good grades. The more they opened up to one another and talked, the more they realized how much they liked each other and how the attributes of one compensated for those of the other. By the time they completed their assignment, Lisa and Sheila had become good friends.

47

The teacher will then ask the following questions:

- ▶ **How did Sheila's and Lisa's friendship develop?**
- ▶ **What are some things you should look for when establishing a good relationship?**
- ▶ **What do you think is a good relationship between people of your age?**
- ▶ **Can people of diverse cultures become friends?**

3. **Identify the Skill Components:** Write the following skill components on the board or on sentence strips:

1. Be always ready to accept new friends.

2. Analyze the meaning of friendship.

3. Decide what you expect from friends.

4. Define the responsibilities friendships impose.

5. Realize that diverse people can form close friendships.

6. Respect each friend's diversity and individuality.

7. Enjoy and nurture friendships.

4. **Model the Skill:** The teacher will portray a youngster of the average age of the class and will ask a student coming from a different culture to role play and befriend her. By using the skill components, the teacher will show how a friendship can be developed.

5. **Behavioral Rehearsal:**

A. *Selection:* The teacher will select four pairs of students to role play.

B. *Role Play:* Each pair of students will role play the following scenarios:

- – The two girls from the story in the introduction.
- – Two students of different background and cultures.
- – One an extroverted student and the other a handicapped student (wheelchair, blind, crippled, etc.)
- – Two students, one with excellent grades and the other with failing grades.

C. *Completion:* After each role play, the teacher will decide if the role play was done correctly and if the skill components were used appropriately. If corrections are needed, the role play will be re-enacted; if not, the role play is complete.

D. *Reinforcers:* The teacher and the class will thank the role players for their participation with applause and verbal compliments.

E. *Discussion:* The teacher will start the discussion by asking the following questions:

- ▶ **How would you start a friendship?**
- ▶ **Whom would you select as a friend? Why?**
- ▶ **Must friends be alike?**
- ▶ **What do you believe is more interesting for two friends, to be alike or different?**
- ▶ **What does friendship mean to you?**

6. **Practice:** Distribute copies of the worksheet "My Friend" for students to complete and discuss in class.

7. **Independent Use:** The teacher will ask the students to complete the "Relationships" worksheet at home and return it in one week, to share in class.

8. **Continuation:** The teacher will emphasize how important friends are during the entire life of a person. Friends can motivate each other to excel in life. Friends frequently are of great help during difficult situations. However, friends can also misguide you and misuse your friendship. Therefore all of us have to be careful in selecting friends.

Name _____ Date _____

MY FRIEND

Directions: In the left column, list the good qualities and behaviors that you think will be needed for a good relationship. In the right column, list behaviors and/or attitudes that in your opinion would end a good relationship. The first one is completed for you.

Desirable Behavior, Attitude, Attribute **Undesirable Behavior, Attitude, Attribute**

1. Respect

2. _____

3. _____

4. _____

5. _____

6. _____

7. _____

8. _____

9. _____

10. _____

1. Anger

2. _____

3. _____

4. _____

5. _____

6. _____

7. _____

8. _____

9. _____

10. _____

Name _____ Date _____

RELATIONSHIPS

Directions: Interview at least five members of your family, friends, or other people that you know and who have a relationship with another person. Based on your interviews, judge which relationships are good ones and which are bad ones. (Do not mention any actual names.) List all attributes such as age, gender, attitudes, behaviors and more for each relationship and then make your judgement.

_____

INTERVIEW #1

_____

INTERVIEW #2

_____

INTERVIEW #3

_____

INTERVIEW #4

_____

INTERVIEW #5

_____

Understanding Boy/Girl Relationships

Behavioral Objective: Children will learn that boy/girl relationships at this age should be in the form of friendship.

Directed Lesson:

1. **Establish the Need:** Today's children are bombarded with adult styles of dress, adult images of intimacy, and, in some cases, adult responsibilities. As early as second grade, they talk about, worry about, and fight about boyfriends/girlfriends. Recently, there was an actual case of a shooting in school because of the loss of a girlfriend. Children should be encouraged to spend their youth learning to be friends independent of gender, which can later be the foundation for mature male/female relationships.

2. **Introduction:** The teacher will read the following story to the class:

   Belinda came home from school a mess . . . her dress was torn, her pony tail was pulled apart, she had some scratches on her face, and some of her homework was missing from her opened bookbag. When her mother saw her, she asked "What happened, Belinda?" in a very worried tone. Belinda explained that Donita had said to her that Brian (from their class) was her, Donita's, boyfriend and that wasn't true because Brian is her boyfriend, so they argued and got into a fight.

   Belinda's mother could not believe what she had just heard . . . her fourth grade daughter was fighting over a boy! But, instead of yelling at Belinda, she kept calm, and asked her how she knew that Brian was her boyfriend and what had happened.

   Belinda said that Brian used to be Donita's boyfriend, but for the past two weeks he had been sitting with her at lunch, holding her hand on the playground, not letting anyone else talk to her—only him, and kissing her hello and goodbye on the mouth. Belinda said that Brian told her he had dumped Donita and that now she was his girlfriend. So, when Donita had said to her that Brian was her boyfriend and to leave him alone, Belinda told her that it was not true and that Brian had dumped her and now was her boyfriend.

   After listening to Belinda, her mother knew that she must have a talk with Belinda right away about how boyfriends/girlfriends should treat each other and when is the right age for other relationships.

   After reading the story, the teacher will ask the following questions to stimulate discussion:

   ▶ **What did Belinda's mother think about Belinda having a boyfriend at her age?**

   ▶ **Was there anything wrong about the way Brian treated Belinda?**

   ▶ **What do you think Belinda's mother will tell her about boyfriend/girlfriend relationships?**

3. *Identify the Skill Components:* List the following skill components on the chalkboard or on a chart.

1. Realize that boyfriend/girlfriend relationships should be based on mutual respect and friendship.

2. Learn how to handle such a relationship without strong involvement.

3. Plan to participate in group activities.

4. Develop the ability to be friends with many peers.

5. Consider appropriate behaviors/activities with boys and girls.

6. Consider the consequences when dating exclusively with a child of different gender.

7. Enjoy many friends.

4. *Model the Skill:* The teacher will play the part of Belinda's mother with a student's help as Belinda. The teacher will use the skill components as a basis for the mother/daughter talk with Belinda.

5. *Behavioral Rehearsal:*

A. *Selection:* The teacher will select students to role play, as needed.

B. *Role Play:* The role players will act out the following scenarios:

- Deshawn's father overhears him talking on the phone to a girl, saying he would like to kiss her "long and hard." Since Deshawn is only nine years old, his father decides that he had better discuss boy/girl relationships with Deshawn.

- Five sixth-grade girls are having a sleep-over at Penny's house. The girls start talking and giggling about boys. Each one reveals that she has a boyfriend. As they each talk about their boyfriend, they find out that they are talking about the same boy. At first they are mad at each other, then they both get mad at him. But Sarah says they really shouldn't be mad at anybody. Sarah says this proves that her mom was right about her being too young for an exclusive boyfriend/girlfriend relationship. Using the skill components, Sara explains what her mother told her.

- Michelle, who is eight years old, is very cute and wears sexy clothes and make-up. She is always talking about boys and how many boyfriends she has. A new boy, Jared, has been in the class for only a few days and Michelle is pressuring him to be her "boyfriend." Jared explains that he will not be a "boyfriend," but that he would like to be a friend.

C. *Completion:* After each role play, the teacher, with the help of the class, will decide if the appropriate behavior was shown. If not, the role play will be re-enacted with corrections. If there are no corrections, the role play is complete.

D. *Reinforcers:* All role playing students will be praised by the teacher for their participation, and all classmates will applaud their efforts.

E. *Discussion:* After each role play, let students discuss what was improper about the relationship and how the skill components were of help. Ask the students if they know of anyone their age who is involved in a too-intimate boyfriend/girlfriend situation and how the skill components could help them develop relationships appropriate for their age.

6. ***Practice:*** Using the following worksheet, "Fun with Friends," the teacher will ask the students to draw a picture of children of their age participating in enjoyable group activities (clubs, choruses, sports, etc.). Under the picture they are to describe what the children are doing and how this helps them to develop friendships.

7. ***Independent Use:*** The teacher will ask the students to copy the skill components on paper and take them home to share with and discuss with their parent(s). Students will be asked to share their parents' comments a week later in class.

8. ***Continuation:*** The teacher will seize opportunities that occur to reinforce the skill. Children should be encouraged to concentrate on developing friendships, to give sufficient time to academic goals, and to increase their individual talents. When they are older, all of these elements will enhance their boyfriend/girlfriend relationships.

Name _____ Date _____

FUN WITH FRIENDS

Directions: In the picture frame, draw a picture of children your age having fun in a group activity. Below, describe what the children are doing and how this will help them develop healthy friendships between girls and boys.

_____

_____

_____

_____

_____

_____

_____

Understanding Rights and Responsibilities

Behavioral Objective: Students will learn that they can exercise their individual rights as citizens only when they are willing to assume responsibility and accountability for their actions and only if in doing so, no harm comes to others.

Directed Lesson:

1. **Establish the Need:** Children claim to have many rights; however, they must learn to realize that these rights can be granted to them only if they are ready and willing to accept the responsibilities that go with the rights. They must understand that no right can be exercised without taking full responsibility; therefore, before being permitted to exercise their rights, they must learn to be fully responsible. They must, also, recognize that rights and responsibilities are required for the purpose of maintaining law and order in society and that rights can only be exercised if they cause no harm to others.

2. **Introduction:** The teacher will read the following statements about "Rights and Responsibilities" to help introduce the skill.

Teachers have the right to:

- ▶ **Be respected by their students.**
- ▶ **Create a safe learning environment.**
- ▶ **Establish, explain, maintain, and enforce classroom rules.**

Teachers have the responsibility to:

- ▶ **Respect the rights and dignity of students, parents, and all other individuals.**
- ▶ **Keep a safe learning environment.**
- ▶ **Establish, maintain, and enforce classroom rules.**

Parents have the right to:

- ▶ **Know what is being taught to their son/daughter.**
- ▶ **Know how their son/daughter is doing in mastering the skills.**
- ▶ **Have a copy of the school's code, or rules of conduct.**
- ▶ **Receive communications informing them of the son's/daughter's progress and all information about school activities.**

Parents have the responsibility to:

- ▶ **Teach the children respect for teachers, adults, and other students.**
- ▶ **Arrange prompt and regular attendance at school for their children.**

> ▶ **Explain the rules of the school to their children.**

> ▶ **Respond to communications from the school.**

Students have the right to:

> ▶ **Be respected by their teacher and other students.**

> ▶ **Have a safe and comfortable learning environment.**

> ▶ **Be told about the rules and consequences for breaking rules.**

> ▶ **Be able to express themselves.**

Students have the responsibility to:

> ▶ **Respect the rights and dignity of other students, teachers, and adults.**

> ▶ **Obey school rules and respect school property.**

> ▶ **Attend school regularly and be on time.**

> ▶ **Conduct themselves in a manner which will not disrupt or deprive others of their education.**

3. ***Identify the skill components:*** The teacher will list the following skill components on a chart or on the chalkboard.

   1. Think about your rights.

   2. Consider the rights of others.

   3. Consider the responsibilities which are associated with each right.

   4. Consider if you have the ability to fulfill the responsibilities.

   5. Remember that you are accountable for your actions.

   6. Determine how to exercise your rights without harming others.

4. ***Model the Skill:*** The teacher will use the example of every citizen of a certain age having the right to drive a car, but only if the person can accept all of the responsibilities that are required to drive a car and is willing to assume accountability for his/her actions. The teacher will use the skill components to illustrate the process of determining rights and responsibilities for driving a car.

5. ***Behavioral Rehearsal:***

   A. *Selection:* The teacher will select three pairs of students to role play.

   B. *Role Play:* In each of the following role plays, one student will discuss the right and the other student will discuss the responsibility.

      – The right to attend school
        The responsibility to follow school rules.

      – The right to express opinions
        The responsibility to do so in a way that does not hurt the feelings or rights of others

      – The right to participate in classroom games
        The responsibility to abide by the rules of the game.

C. *Completion:* After each role play, the teacher will reinforce correct behaviors, identify inappropriate behaviors, and have the role play re-enacted with corrections, if necessary. If there are no corrections, the role play is complete.

D. *Reinforcers:* The teacher will use an acceptable method to reward the role-playing students for their cooperation.

E. *Discussion:* The teacher will ask the students to suggest other rights and responsibilities that go together.

6. **Practice:** The teacher will pass out the worksheet "Classroom Rights," for students to complete. As a class exercise, the children and the teacher will select rights and responsibilities to be placed on the "classroom rights" chart, which will be posted in the classroom as a reminder.

7. **Independent Use:** The teacher will send home the worksheet "Home Rights. In this worksheet the teacher asks the students' parents to help them fill out their worksheet in regard to home rights. Children will share and discuss their completed worksheets in school one week later.

8. **Continuation:** Further discussions about rights and responsibilities can take place as the opportunity presents itself. The teacher will continue to point out that rights and responsibilities go "hand in hand."

Name _____ Date _____

CLASSROOM RIGHTS

Bill of RIGHTS

Directions: List the rights that you feel are due to children in this classroom and then list the responsibilities related to each right.

Rights	Responsibility
1.	1.
2.	2.
3.	3.
4.	4.
5.	5.

Name _____ Date _____

HOME RIGHTS

Dear Parent:

Please help your child select four rights that he/she has as a member of your family and then have him/her determine what responsibilities are associated with that right. Ask your child to record the rights and responsibilities on this sheet and please sign your name.

Rights	Responsibility
Parent _____	
1. _____	1. _____
2. _____	2. _____
3. _____	3. _____
4. _____	4. _____
5. _____	5. _____

Learning the Importance of Rules

Behavioral Objective: Students will learn to understand that it is necessary to have rules to provide order in all areas of our life and how to comply with these rules.

Directed Lesson:

1. **Establish the Need:** Children initially believe that they would be happier without any restrictions, but find that life is easier when there are rules which they can follow. By following rules, fighting and other aggressive acts can be settled in a peaceful manner. Children need to realize that if they follow rules, they will have a more peaceful environment and more time for learning and play.

2. **Introduction:** The teacher will read the following story to the class.

    > On the first day of school when Mr. Brown started to present the classroom rules to the class, the children complained about having rules. They said they were third graders and old enough to know the rules. So, Mr. Brown decided to let them go without rules for two weeks providing that they would behave appropriately.

    > Soon there was chaos in the classroom. Emmett and Joe started fighting; each child wanted to be first in line; children walked around the room whenever they felt like it; everyone spoke at the same time trying to out-shout each other; and Mary started eating her lunch each day around 11:00 A.M.

    > No one gave attention to the teacher or to each other.

    The teacher will use the following questions to discuss the situation in Mr. Brown's classroom:

    ▶ **How do you think the children in Mr. Brown's class feel about the chaos?**

    ▶ **What do you think Mr. Brown should do?**

    ▶ **Why do you think rules are needed?**

3. **Skill Components:** The teacher will list the following skill components on a chart or the chalkboard.

    1. Consider the situation.

    2. Understand the consequences of not having rules.

    3. Think about rules that would provide orderly and peaceful co-existence.

    4. Consider the rules which are needed.

    5. Accept the rules.

    6. Follow the rules.

4. ***Model the Skill:*** The teacher will show the class how the fight between Emmett and Joe could have been avoided if there had been classroom rules. The teacher will use the skill components to convey the importance of having rules.

5. ***Behavioral Rehearsal:***

   A. *Selection:* The teacher will select the appropriate number of students needed for the following role plays.

   B. *Role Plays:* The children will role play the following scenarios:

      – Mary, Jacob and Frances want to go to the restroom at the same time. There is only one restroom pass.

      – Adam was told to go directly to the store to buy milk and come right back home. Instead, on the way home, Adam stopped at a friend's house and played for an hour.

      – David always runs through the halls, which are usually crowded. Today, he collided with Harry, who became angry.

      – The substitute teacher was having a difficult time with the children. They were noisy and were not following the posted class rules.

   C. *Completion:* After each role play the teacher and class will determine if the role play was done correctly. If not, the behaviors to be corrected will be identified and the role play re-enacted. If yes, the role play is complete.

   D. *Reinforcers:* The teacher will show appreciation for the role players' efforts through appropriate rewards and applause.

   E. *Discussion:* The teacher will ask the children to discuss which school rules help them to get along better and to perform better academically. The children will be asked to discuss their home rules and why they are necessary at home and how they promote harmony in the family.

6. ***Practice:*** The teacher will distribute the worksheet "Up with School Rules," which children will complete in class and then share their responses.

7. ***Independent Use:*** The children will be given the "Up with Family Rules" sheet to take home and complete after discussing family rules with their parents.

8. ***Continuation:*** The teacher will stress the fact that rules make life better by providing order and peaceful solutions in all areas of everyday living. She/he will remind the children that when they get older they will have more input into the rules which govern their families, workplace and government; so, it is to their advantage to learn which rules are needed and how the rules will benefit them and society.

Name _____ Date _____

UP WITH SCHOOL RULES

Directions: Draw a picture about one of your school rules that you think is very important. Write the rule under your picture then tell why you think it is important.

School Rule:

_____

_____

_____

This school rule is important because: _____

_____

_____

_____

_____

Name _____ Date _____

UP WITH FAMILY RULES

Directions: Discuss with your parents some of the rules you have in your family. Choose one that you think is very important. Draw a picture of that rule. Under the picture of the rule, write the rule and explain why this family rule is important. Have one of your parents sign this sheet.

Family Rule:

_____

_____

_____

This family rule is important because: _____

_____

_____

_____

_____

Parent

Achieving Family Harmony

Behavioral Objective: Children will learn how to contribute to family harmony through the understanding of others and the use of communication and listening skills.

Directed Lesson:

1. ***Establish the Need:*** The number of dysfunctional families in our society has increased significantly during the last two decades. But even in normal families strife can be brought about by economic factors as well as the usual problems of inadequate communication and listening skills and general disrespect for others. The development of adequate communication and listening skills is integral to family harmony as well as to success in school and in life.

2. ***Introduction:*** The teacher will read the following story to the class:

   > **Karen is 8 years old and her sister Joan is 16. Although they are nearly a decade apart in age, Joan is very close to Karen and looks out for her welfare. Joan has a well-paying job after school and on weekends and is able to buy Karen gifts of clothing and toys beyond what their parents can provide.**

   > **One day, Joan and Karen were at the mall when Karen saw a doll she wanted. Karen told Joan that their parents couldn't afford to purchase it for her, but that she would really like to have it. What she didn't tell Joan was that her mother had reminded her not to ask Joan to buy it for her.**

   > **When Joan offered to buy the doll for her, Karen was very excited. She told Joan that she "loved it and loved Joan."**

   > **When they arrived home, a very excited Karen ran to her mother shouting "Look what Joan gave me!"**

   The teacher will ask the following questions:

   - ◗ **How do you think the mother will react?**
   - ◗ **How will this incident affect the family harmony?**
   - ◗ **Was there another way that Karen could have gotten the doll from Joan without disobeying her mother?**
   - ◗ **Even after the doll was purchased, was there a better way for Karen to tell her mother about the doll?**

3. ***Identify the Skill Components:*** The teacher will write the following skill components on a chart, sentence strips or chalkboard.

1. Remember family rules.
2. Be respectful of family members.
3. Communicate often and clearly with family members.
4. Listen to what other family members have to say.
5. Consider how your actions will affect the family's harmony.
6. Act in the best interest of all family members.

4. ***Model the Skill:*** The teacher will role play Peter, age 12 and will ask a student to role play his sister, Emma, age nine. Both children have weekly chores: each weekend Peter cleans the garage and Emma does the dishes on Friday, Saturday and Sunday. Emma constantly complains that her job is harder than Peter's and this is not fair. Using the skill components, Peter will communicate to Emma what his job entails compared to her job, thus maintaining family harmony and Emma will no longer complain.

5. ***Behavioral Rehearsal:***

   A. *Selection:* The teacher will select three groups of children to participate in the role plays.

   B. *Role Plays:* The role plays will be enacted by the children using the skill components to keep harmony in the family.

   – Karen, Joan and Mother from the story in the introduction.

   – Thomas, Mary and Kelly all want to use the computer at the same time. Kelly, being the oldest, helps to maintain harmony among the three of them.

   – Father is away on a business trip. Mother, Kevin and Alice are at home. Kevin wishes to go to a soccer practice and Alice wants to go swimming. The mother asks them to agree either to go to the game or swimming together since she can take them to one place only. That is all the time she has.

   C. *Completion:* After each role play, the teacher and class will determine if the role play was done correctly. If not, the role play will be re-enacted with corrections. If yes, the role play is complete.

   D. *Reinforcers:* The teacher and class members will applaud profusely each group of role players.

   E. *Discussion:* The teacher will ask if anyone would like to describe a troublesome actual family situation and the outcome. If not all parties involved were satisfied and the family harmony was disrupted, how could using the skill components help to bring harmony to the family?

6. ***Practice:*** The teacher will ask the students to complete the worksheet "Creating Family Harmony" in class and share their answers. NOTE: The teacher should discuss the meaning of each word on the worksheet, along with its pronunciation, with the class before giving the assignment.

7. ***Independent Use:*** The teacher will hand out the worksheet "Family Flash" to be completed and returned to class in one week for sharing and discussion.

8. ***Continuation:*** The teacher will remind children that all members of the family can participate in creating harmony in the family. If family members can get along better within the family, they will be able to take that skill with them as they go to school, play and interact with other people.

Name _____ Date _____

CREATING FAMILY HARMONY

Directions: Fill in the missing words to show how you can help create harmony in your family. Use the words at the bottom of the page. Reviewing the skill components will help you.

1. Remember family _____ and _____.

2. Be _____ of family members.

3. _____ often and _____ with family members.

4. _____ to what other family members have to say.

5. Consider how _____ _____ will affect the family's harmony.

6. _____ in the _____ _____ of all family members.

Use these words. One does not belong. Why?

listen   actions

expectations   best

argue   rules

communicate   respectful

act   clearly

interest   your

Name _____ Date _____

CREATING FAMILY HARMONY
Answer Key

Directions: Fill in the missing words to show how you can help create harmony in your family. Use the words at the bottom of the page. Reviewing the skill components will help you.

1. Remember family ____rules____ and ____expectations____.

2. Be ____respectful____ of family members.

3. ____Communicate____ often and ____clearly____ with family members.

4. ____Listen____ to what other family members have to say.

5. Consider how ____your____ ____actions____ will affect the family's harmony.

6. ____Act____ in the ____best____ ____interest____ of all family members.

Use these words. One does not belong. Why?

listen   actions

expectations   best

argue   rules

communicate   respectful

act   clearly

interest   your

Name _____   Date _____

FAMILY FLASH

Listening

Directions: On three separate sheets of paper, draw a picture of family harmony as it relates to:

1. Listening
2. Respect
3. Communications

Write one or two sentences under the picture on each page which describes what is happening.

Respect

Communications

Understanding Stress in the Family

Behavioral Objective: Children will learn how to cope with stress in the family which can create disruptive or violent behaviors by one or more family members.

Directed Lesson:

1. **Establish the Need:** Children need to understand that many stresses in the family are influenced by situations outside the family, such as loss of a job or having to move. Stress can cause changes in behavior, such as becoming very nervous, irritable, angry, and starting to drink, shout, etc. Children will be best able to cope with such situations by being tolerant, forgiving and supportive. In order to deal with some stressful situations, children may need to seek help from a parent or other trusted adult.

2. **Introduction:** The teacher will read the following story to introduce a stressful family situation:

> **After working for the same company for 18 years, Marilyn's father lost his job two months ago because the company went out-of-business. Marilyn's mother went back to work as a secretary to support the family. Losing his job and having his wife support the family has made Marilyn's father feel very useless and depressed. He has not tried to find another job but sits at home all day staring at the TV. He used to be a lot of fun; he would spend time with Marilyn, help her with homework, and didn't mind her friends or hearing their music. Now, he says he doesn't have time for Marilyn and that her friends and the music are too loud. Lately, he has been getting angry and seems to argue with Marilyn's mother over every little thing. Marilyn has not been sleeping well and her mother seems nervous and is losing weight.**

> **Marilyn doesn't understand why her father has changed so much and asks her mother what is happening to her father and when he will be his "old" self again. Her mother explains that he is feeling depressed because of losing his job and has changed only temporarily. Mother tells Marilyn that they both must let her father know they still love him and know that he is smart and a good worker. Mother encourages Marilyn by assuring her that they, as a family, will get through this and that she will talk with father about going to a job counselor.**

The teacher will emphasize that situations similar to that in Marilyn's family puts stress on all members of the family and will ask what the word "stress" means. (A suitable description could be: "Stress is a state of mind (how you feel) when certain situations or happenings cause a person to be under extra pressure . . . stress can affect the way a person thinks, feels, behaves and can cause health problems") Then ask:

> ◗ **What is causing the stress in Marilyn's family?**
> ◗ **How is the stress affecting Father? Mother? Marilyn?**
> ◗ **How can Marilyn cope with the stress?**

3. *Identify the Skill Components:* The teacher will list the skill components on a chart or chalkboard.

1. Decide if your family is being stressed.

2. Think about how the stress is affecting each member.

3. Determine what the cause of the stress is.

4. Discuss your feelings with a parent or trusted adult.

5. Think what you can do to help a stressed family member.

4. *Model the Skill:* The teacher will role play Marilyn from the story in the introduction to model how to use the skill components to cope with such a situation. The "think aloud" method could be used.

5. *Behavioral Rehearsal:*

A. *Selection:* The teacher will select an appropriate number of students to participate in the following role plays.

B. *Role Plays:* The following stressful situations could be placed on index cards and passed out to the role playing students.

- Beverly lives with her grandmother and sees her mother only several times a year. Sometimes her mother will call, promise to visit and tell Beverly she is bringing toys and clothes for Beverly; then, Mother doesn't come to visit at all. This makes Beverly's grandmother very angry and Beverly feels upset and alone. When this happens, Beverly's grades at school go down for a few weeks.

- Bill has learned, at school, that chemical substances such as alcohol, cigarettes and drugs are very harmful. He worries a lot about his mother because she constantly smokes cigarettes. He worries so much, he gets headaches when he thinks about the harmful effects of smoking.

- Nick and his brother are hearing yet another fight between their parents. They always make sure to stay out of the way when their parents fight. This time, they hear their mother say she is getting a divorce.

- David really loves his older brother Darryl; but, whenever something goes wrong for Darryl, such as earning a poor grade on a test or having an argument with his girlfriend, Darryl uses David as a punching bag. David always has bruises on his body.

C. *Completion:* After each role play, the teacher and class will determine if the role play was done correctly. If not, the role play will be re-enacted with corrections. If yes, the role play is complete.

D. *Reinforcers:* The teacher and class will show their support of the role players with generous applause and praise.

E. *Discussion:* The teacher will stimulate a discussion about stressful family situations with the following questions:

> ❱ **Do you think all families experience some type of stress? What kind?**
>
> ❱ **Why are some families better able to cope with stressful situations?**
>
> ❱ **To whom could a family or family members go for help?**

6. *Practice:* The teacher will distribute the worksheet "Stressed Out" for students to complete in class and then share correct answers.

NOTE: Be sure to discuss the meaning of the words with the children before they start the assignment.

7. *Independent Use:* The teacher will have the children take home the worksheet "A Family Problem." The children should be encouraged to read the story with their parents, discuss the items A, B and C and complete the worksheets. When the worksheet is returned to school, children can share their responses.

8. *Continuation:* The teacher will reinforce the fact that stress in the family is often caused by factors which are beyond the control of children. However, children can learn to recognize what stress is, how it affects family members, what caused it, and what they can do to cope with the changed behavior due to stress.

Name _____   Date _____

STRESSED OUT

Directions: Use the words below to fill in the missing words in the sentences about family stress.

recognize	stress
problems	adult
violent	parent
cope	behavior
health	differently

1. Many different kinds of _____ can cause _____ in the family.

2. Too much stress can affect a person's _____ and _____.

3. Stress can cause family members to behave _____, even become _____.

4. You can learn to _____ the signs of stress in the family.

5. Then, you can discuss your concerns with a _____ or other trusted _____.

6. With help, you can learn to _____ with stressful family situations.

Name _____ Date _____

STRESSED OUT
Answer Key

Directions: Use the words below to fill in the missing words in the sentences about family stress.

recognize	stress
problems	adult
violent	parent
cope	behavior
health	differently

1. Many different kinds of ____problems____ can cause ____stress____ in the family.

2. Too much stress can affect a person's ____health____ and ____behavior____.

3. Stress can cause family members to behave ____differently____, even become ____violent____.

4. You can learn to ____recognize____ the signs of stress in the family.

5. Then, you can discuss your concerns with a ____parent____ or other trusted ____adult____.

6. With help, you can learn to ____cope____ with stressful family situations.

Name _____ Date _____

A Family Problem

Pretend That:

Mother slipped in the kitchen and broke her hip. She will be in the hospital for 2 weeks and then in a rehabilitation center for 4 weeks to strengthen her muscles so she can walk again.

While she is recuperating, Father has been trying to go to work each day, take care of the house, cook, wash clothes and get you, age 10, and your brother, age 5, and your sister, age 12, off to school each morning. All you children have done is whine about the fact the he does not do things like Mother. After three weeks of this he has a very short temper, is very tired and constantly complains of a headache.

A. What are the signs that Father is feeling stressed?

1. _____

2. _____

3. _____

B. Why do you think Father is stressed and how can you reduce some of Father's stress.

_____

_____

_____

C. Name as many things as you can think of that the children in the family could do that would show love, help and support for father.

_____

_____

_____

D. What kinds of stress are the children experiencing?

_____

_____

_____

E. What do you think the children should do to reduce the stress they are experiencing?

_____

_____

_____

Understanding Sibling Rivalry

Behavioral Objective: Children will learn to accept that brothers/sisters, or siblings, require different amounts of attention at various stages of their life and that the attention a sibling receives from the parents should not lead to jealousy and disrupt good family relationships.

Directed Lesson:

1. **Establish the Need:** It is important for children to understand that siblings receive different amounts of attention, praise, privileges, and so on according to the needs of a child based on his/her age and physical, mental and emotional conditions. Sometimes, children misinterpret the actions of the parents towards other children in the family; when this happens, it can lead to jealousy, acting out and disruption for the whole family. Children must learn to realize the needs of other children in the family and to accept being treated differently as long as their needs are met in the knowledge that parents have equal love for all their children.

2. **Introduction:** The teacher will read the following story to the class:

> Tami is eight years old and is the second child in the family. Other children include Paul, a thirteen-year-old brother, a five-year-old brother, Tommy, and a three-month-old baby girl named Renee.

> Tami's friend, Sally, has come to play for the afternoon. Tami's mother puts the baby, Renee, in the playpen in the living room where Tami and Sally are playing. Sally stops playing with Tami and starts playing with Renee, making silly noises and giggling with the baby. Tami feels as though she has become invisible.

> As Sally continues to play with Renee, Tami slumps on the sofa and thinks about just how invisible and miserable she feels.

> Paul is always being praised by their parents because he is a good athlete and he gets to stay up until 10 P.M. and Tami has to go to bed at 8:30 P.M., the same time as her little brother! Tommy is in kindergarten this year and every paper he brings home from school is put on the refrigerator like it is so-o-o special! There is no room for her school work. When Tami looks at the baby, tears begin to form in her eyes. There is *her* friend Sally playing with Renee instead of her. Everybody plays with the baby! And, when the baby is asleep, Mother is always reminding Tami to be quiet. In fact, that's all mother does—do for, talk about, and worry about, THE BABY!! Mother used to read to her every day and put her artwork on the refrigerator and let her play the piano for fun—but not anymore. Tami thinks to herself, "Why did that baby have to be born? Everybody thinks Paul is so great because he can kick a dumb football. And Tommy's papers look like a bunch of scribble marks, so why do they get displayed?" The tears spill out of her eyes and flow down her cheeks.

> She is so unhappy that the thought of suicide crosses her mind.

After a brief pause to allow the children to consider how Tami is feeling, the teacher will ask the following questions:

▶ **What is Tami feeling? (these feelings could be listed on the chalkboard as the children name them)**

▶ **Who do you think she blames for the way she feels?**

▶ **Do you think her parents know how she feels?**

The teacher will then state that many children "go through" what Tami is experiencing. When they do not understand why things are as they are, children can make the situation worse by becoming very jealous, acting bad, getting in trouble, not doing their school work, etc. Competition for parents' attention, or sibling rivalry, is the problem. Here are some skill components that could help Tami or other children to understand and deal with sibling rivalry.

3. *Identify the Skill Components:* List on the chalkboard or a chart:

1. Decide why you are feeling jealous.
2. Consider why you believe that your siblings are getting more attention than you.
3. Consider the needs for siblings of different ages.
4. Study your own behavior.
5. Decide if you need to improve your self-image.
6. Remember that parents love all their children equally.
7. Discuss your feelings and ideas with your parent(s).
8. Develop understanding for all members in the family.

4. *Model the Skill:* If the teacher can recall an incident of sibling rivalry from his/her own past, this can be related to the children with an explanation of how the skill components could be applied. If not, the teacher could model Tami using the skill components to find a way to change her situation and feelings.

5. *Behavioral Rehearsal:*

A. *Selection:* The teacher will divide the class into four teams of students to role play the following incidents of sibling rivalry.

B. *Role Plays:* Each team will role play their example of sibling rivalry. To decide what the problem is and how to resolve it they will be using the skill components. They will need to assign roles to selected team members.

   – David is 10 years old and has a 9:00 P.M. bedtime. His 14-year-old brother gets to stay up until 10:30 P.M. David doesn't think this is fair and cries and complains almost every evening. Sometimes he has tantrums and starts fighting.

   – Cheyenne is in the second grade. Her younger sister, Buffy, is not yet in school. Cheyenne is very upset (jealous) that Buffy gets to stay home with mother while she has to go to school. She is so upset that she slaps Buffy just to get even.

   – Maria and Mario are eight-year-old twins. Their parents don't know what to do. Maria and Mario are always saying the parents love one more than the other. If Mother buys a new dress for Maria, Mario complains that mother is *always* buying stuff for Maria. When Daddy takes Mario to Little League practice, Maria whines and stomps around the house. Because of the jealousy they fight often.

– Andy, who is 12 years old, has several chores that he is responsible for every day. His sister Kate is eight years old and in Andy's opinion is a spoiled brat . . . she doesn't have to do anything! All she does is make her bed, does her homework and practices the piano for 1/2 hour. He does those things plus he feeds and walks the dog, takes out the garbage and on weekends helps with the lawn care. For this reason he does not like his sister and is very rough with her.

C. *Completion:* After each role play, the teacher and class will reinforce the correct behaviors, identify inappropriate behaviors and ask the students to re-enact the role plays with corrections if necessary. If there are no corrections, the role play is complete.

D. *Reinforcers:* The teacher will give praise to the teams for their input, cooperation and role playing ability.

E. *Discussion:* After the role plays, the teacher will ask a spokesperson for each team to explain why they performed the role play as they did. The teacher will ask the other class members if they had a different approach to resolve the sibling rivalry. The teacher could also ask the class if anyone has experienced this kind of sibling rivalry (or knows someone who did) and if or how it was resolved.

6. **Practice:** The teacher will have student complete the "Jealous Tears" worksheet and share the correct answers when finished.

7. **Independent Use:** The teacher will distribute the worksheet entitled "Resolving Sibling Rivalry" and ask the students to address the letter, sign their name and fill in the name of a sibling and why they may be feeling jealous of that sibling. They will then share the letter with the addressee and discuss a resolution using the skill components. The student should write a brief explanation of how the sibling rivalry was resolved.

8. **Continuation:** The teacher will assure children that sibling rivalry is a part of growing up and having the ability to deal with it will help them to feel happier and get along better with siblings. This skill can be transferred to help people deal with jealousy of friends and can even help them after they become adults.

Name _____ Date _____

JEALOUS TEARS

Directions: Help Tami to understand sibling rivalry. Fill in the missing words. Choose these words to complete the sentences:

Love	**Child**	**Attention**
Understand	**Sibling**	**Jealous**
Parents	**Family**	**Skill**
Rivalry	**Components**	

1. S_____ R_____ happens when one child in the F_____ is J_____ of another child.

2. It is important to remember that P_____ are able to L_____ all their children equally.

3. It is important to U_____ that at certain times one C_____ may need more A_____.

4. If you are feeling J_____ of a sister or brother, use the S_____ C_____ to help resolve the S_____ R_____.

5. Write down the Skill Components.

1. _____

2. _____

3. _____

4. _____

5. _____

6. _____

7. _____

8. _____

Name _____ Date _____

JEALOUS TEARS
Answer Key

Directions: Help Tami to understand sibling rivalry. Fill in the missing words. Choose these words to complete the sentences:

Love	Child	Attention
Understand	Sibling	Jealous
Parents	Family	Skill
Rivalry	Components	

1. S_ibling_ R_ivalry_ happens when one child in the F_amily_ is J_ealous_ of another child.

2. It is important to remember that P_arents_ are able to L_ove_ all their children equally.

3. It is important to U_nderstand_ that at certain times one C_hild_ may need more A_ttention_.

4. If you are feeling J_ealous_ of a sister or brother, use the S_kill_ C_omponents_ to help resolve the S_ibling_ R_ivalry_.

Name _____ Date _____

Resolving Sibling Rivalry

Directions: Below is a letter to your Mom, Dad or whoever you choose to help you to get a better understanding of your jealousy towards your sibling(s). Fill in the missing words and discuss the letter with the person to whom you address it and who gets the letter.

Dear _____:

In my classroom, we have discussed sibling rivalry and how to resolve it in an appropriate manner using the following skill components:

1. Decide why you are feeling jealous.
2. Consider why you believe that your siblings are getting more attention than you.
3. Consider the needs for siblings of different ages.
4. Study your own behavior.
5. Decide if you need to improve your self-image.
6. Remember that parents love all their children equally.
7. Discuss your feelings and ideas with your parent(s).
8. Develop understanding for all members in the family.

I would like to discuss with you some jealous feelings I have toward _____

_____ because _____

_____

_____

_____

Thank you for your help.

Your Child

_____

In the space below, explain how this sibling rivalry was resolved.

_____

_____

_____

_____

_____

_____

Understanding Elderly Family Members

Behavioral Objective: Students will learn to understand the needs of the elderly and how to help elderly family members, especially if they live at the same house.

Directed Lesson:

1. **Establish the Need:** Sometimes, children must adjust to having an elderly relative move into their family's home. Routines, habits, activities and allocated space often have to change to accommodate the needs of the elderly relative who may need assistance for such elementary tasks as eating, dressing and so on, due to diminished mental and/or physical capabilities. Children need to learn about the elderly person's limitations. Children must be taught that the elderly deserve their respect, kindness, and assistance, and to realize that a mutual friendship can develop. Young and old alike will be able to join in interesting activities, share information and learn from each other.

2. **Introduction:** The teacher will read the following story to the class:

   Robert, a fifth grader, and Sandra, a third grader, lived with their parents in a three-bedroom house. Their grandmother who was 65 years old, had come to live with them while she was recovering from a broken hip. Since there were only three bedrooms, the family room became Grandmother's bedroom.

   Robert and Sandra were quite upset because the family room was where they watched TV, played games, played with their friends and did their homework. They had to use the kitchen table for homework and watch TV on a very small television set which was on the kitchen counter. Friends could only play at their house if they could play outside. When they complained, Mother and Dad told them that sometimes we have to make small sacrifices to help someone; and, Grandmother really needed their help and because she was an important person and they loved her so much, everyone should do their part to make her feel welcome.

   As Grandmother began to feel better and started to use a walker, she began to encourage Robert and Sandra to join her to watch TV on the big TV set. She would let them sit on her hospital bed, while she read to them, which they liked because this bed could go up and down! Grandmother told them every day that she felt so much better when they kept her company. Some days, Grandmother would tell them stories about when their father was a little boy, which they enjoyed.

   When Robert went to the library, Grandmother would tell him which book she would like to read; Robert would bring the book for Grandmother. When Grandmother needed a drink and a snack, Sandra felt quite grown-up serving her.

One day, Robert and Sandra told their parents that it was nice to have Grandmother living with them. They asked their parents if some friends could come over to meet Grandmother.

After reading the story, the teacher will ask these questions:

▶ **How do you think Grandmother felt about having a broken hip and not being able to live in her own house?**

▶ **What were Grandmother's physical limitations?**

▶ **IIow did Robert and Sandra's feelings about Grandmother living with them change? Why?**

▶ **How did this story demonstrate that young people and old people can get along?**

▶ **If Grandmother's hip heals enough so that she can live in her own house again, how do you think Robert and Sandra will feel?**

3. *Identify the Skill Components:* The teacher will write the skill components on a chart or chalkboard.

1. Try to understand the elderly person's feelings.

2. Think about the needs of the elderly person.

3. Discuss any negative feelings with your parent.

4. Realize that sharing information is gaining knowledge.

5. Share in caring for them.

6. Show patience, kindness and understanding.

7. Feel good about yourself when you respect the elderly.

4. *Model the Skill:* The teacher will model the use of the skill components through the "think aloud" method to demonstrate how he/she as a child, would react to an elderly relative who is bedridden and constantly asking for things to be brought to the bed.

5. *Behavioral Rehearsal:*

A. *Selection:* The teacher will select the appropriate number of students for the following role plays:

B. *Role Plays:*

– From the story in the introduction about Grandmother, the parents will use the skill components to help Robert and Sandra understand the situation.

– Gerrie hears Bernard making fun of her (Gerrie's) grandfather because he has difficulty remembering things. Grandfather is 70 years old. Gerrie helps Bernard to understand the elderly grandfather by using the skill components.

C. *Completion:* Following the role play, the teacher will reinforce correction behaviors and identify and re-enact inappropriate behaviors, if needed. If there are no corrections, role play is complete.

    D. *Reinforcers:* Role players will receive appropriate praise and/or rewards from the teacher.

    E. *Discussion:* After the role plays, the teacher will ask the students if any of them have elderly relatives living with them (or had in the past) and to describe the changes that had to be made to accommodate these persons. The teacher will also discuss what kinds of things a child of their age can do to make the relatives feel welcome, etc.

6. ***Practice:*** The teacher will have the students complete the worksheet "Time Together" and share their responses.

7. ***Independent Use:*** The teacher will hand out the worksheet "Young and Old—How Do We Compare" which students will complete at home and return to school. Students should be encouraged to involve their parents in completing this assignment. Their responses can be shared in class.

8. ***Continuation:*** The teacher will remind students that elderly persons are not the only ones who may need special care, assistance, and consideration. Persons of all ages with temporary or permanent injuries or handicaps may require similar attention. When providing such care, the students will realize that they gain much satisfaction, increased self-esteem, insight and enjoyment by sharing their time in this way.

Name _____ Date _____

TIME TOGETHER

Directions: Think of two activities that you and an elderly person could do together. Then tell how doing this activity together will help each person.

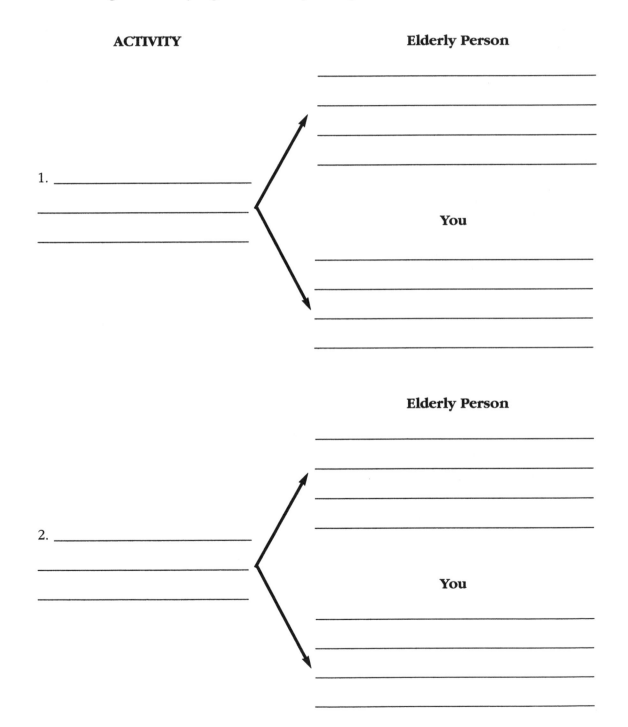

ACTIVITY

Elderly Person

1. _____

_____

_____

You

Elderly Person

2. _____

_____

_____

You

Name _____ Date _____

YOUNG AND OLD—HOW DO WE COMPARE?

Directions: Complete the following table of information by describing in brief statements how the young and the old are the same and different in each category and in feelings and needs.

How are you	Same?	Different?	Because of the Difference, What Can You Do to Help?
APPEARANCE			
HEALTH			
KNOWLEDGE			
PHYSICAL ABILITY			
EXPERIENCE(S)			
HAPPINESS			

FEELINGS

SELF-WORTH			
LOVE			

NEEDS

FOOD			
CLOTHING			
SHELTER			
PERSONAL			

Understanding Family Fights

Behavioral Objective: Students will learn that family fights can be physical as well as verbal and can be frequently avoided and stopped when the family understands the reasons why they occur and uses appropriate skills to cope.

Directed Lesson:

1. ***Establish the Need:*** Unfortunately fights in families are frequent and can create great anxiety and trauma, especially in children who often are innocent bystanders. All family members must learn to understand the reasons why those emotional excesses occur and lead to physical fights and cursing. Causes for these fights, if fully comprehended, can frequently be lessened or fully removed. If that is not possible, skills have to be learned to cope with the emotional reactions to those causes.

2. ***Introduction:*** The teacher will read the following story to the class:

   The McDonald family appeared to be a loving family. And maybe they did love one another, but behind closed doors there was a lot happening that made Donald, age 8, very unhappy. He had an abusive father who would throw his dinner plate if the food was not done just right. Donald could not believe it. His mother worked all day just like his father and when she came home she would go straight to the kitchen and start dinner. At first, when the father threw the dinner plate, his mother would just pick up the plate and clean the floor. When the father continued to throw things more often, she started yelling back at him and sometimes they would hit each other. Donald did not blame his mother for getting angry, but he was becoming really nervous about all the fighting.

   Also Donald's father would yell at him for not turning off a light or playing his music loudly. Lately, he had started to spank Donald really hard, which caused a bruise on his arm and a black eye.

   The teacher will lead a discussion with the following questions:

   ▶ **Predict what will happen to this family.**

   ▶ **Why do you think the father is behaving so violently?**

   ▶ **How do you think Donald was feeling?**

   ▶ **Why do you think violence occurs so frequently?**

   ▶ **Is violence always physical?**

   ▶ **How else can violence be expressed?**

3. ***Identify the Skill Components:*** Write the following skill components on the board or on sentence strips.

   1. Consider reasons that cause violent family exchanges.

   2. Take into account the frequency of these acts.

   3. Consider the serious consequences.

   4. Consider how these violent actions affect you and others.

   5. Think of everybody's feelings.

   6. Think of means to stop the violence.

   7. Decide if you need help.

   8. Ask for help, if needed.

   9. Make a plan.

4. ***Model the Skill:*** The teacher will tell about an actual family she knows where violence is a problem or make up such a family. The teacher will use the skill components to show how they could help to understand the problem.

5. ***Behavioral Rehearsal:***

   A. *Selection:* The teacher will select three groups of students to role play.

   B. *Role Plays:* Each of the groups will role play one of the following scenarios:

      – Donald, the mother and the father from the story in the introduction.

      – Anne's older brother hit her and her sister. When she told her parents about it, they did nothing.

      – An uncle who visits frequently beats the children Bob and Maurice, ages 8 and 10, and challenges the mother to do the same.

   C. *Completion:* After each role play, reinforce correct behavior, identify inappropriate behavior and re-enact with corrections. If there are no corrections, role play is complete.

   D. *Reinforcers:* The teacher will compliment the students about their role playing and thank them profusely. The class will give great applause.

   E. *Discussion:* The teacher will lead a discussion with the class about fighting in the family. This could include the reasons for fighting, who is abused and who could help. The discussion could also include the feelings of different family members and how the conflicts could be resolved without fights.

6. ***Practice:*** The teacher will distribute the worksheet "Stop the Violence" and ask the students to complete it in class and share their answers with their classmates.

7. ***Independent Use:*** The teacher will distribute the worksheet "Peaceful" to be completed at home and returned in one week for discussion in class.

8. ***Continuation:*** The teacher will reiterate at any opportunity that violent outbreaks are not permissible no matter what age the person is, and that all conflicts, no matter how serious, can be dealt with by using skills as learned in this lesson.

Name _____   Date _____

STOP THE VIOLENCE

Directions: Write a paragraph about two instances of family violence, one physical and the other verbal, and give a reason why each might have occurred and how you suggest it can be stopped.

1. Physical Violence: _____

_____

_____

_____

Reason: _____

How to Stop: _____

_____

_____

2. Verbal Violence: _____

_____

_____

_____

Reason: _____

How to Stop: _____

_____

_____

Name _____ Date _____

PEACEFUL

Directions: Write words that a loving peaceful family would use with each other. Discuss these words with your parent(s). Then write a story of a family where all family members pull together to solve a violent conflict peacefully. (Use the skill components.)

Words used by family members:

_____ _____ _____ _____

_____ _____ _____ _____

A story of a family conflict which starts violently and is solved peacefully.

_____

_____

_____

_____

_____

_____

_____

Which skill component did you use? Write in skill components you used.

1. _____   5. _____

2. _____   6. _____

3. _____   7. _____

4. _____   8. _____

Understanding Early Signs of Troublesome Situations

Behavioral Objective: Children will learn that a troubled and dangerous situation is frequently preceded by warning signs and that it is most important to spot these signs early and to learn the skills to react to them cleverly in order to avoid the violence that is possible to occur.

Directed Lesson:

1. ***Establish the Need:*** Frequently, troublesome situations are preceded by warning signs and can be avoided when recognizing those signs. Children can be trained to spot those signs before a dangerous situation explodes by giving close attention to what is said and done. After understanding these warnings, the students have to learn how to react cleverly and appropriately to avoid the danger to come. Every situation will be different and the children will have to practice the skills to learn how to react properly.

2. ***Introduction:*** The teacher will read the following story to the class:

   > **On weekends Alex and David usually go to the playground to play a game of "pick up" basketball. There are always several boys on the playground and you can count on a good time. One Saturday there were some new boys and they seemed nice so they played ball.**

   > **As the game was being played Alex noticed that the new boys used a lot of curse words and would give unnecessary "pushes."**

   > **When the game was winding down, one of the new boys came to Alex and said "You think you are so tough." Alex realized that this boy might start trouble, so he replied "It was nice playing with you." Then he turned to David and said "Come on David, we have to get home—I'm late."**

   The teacher will ask the following questions:

   ▶ **What do you think the new boy wanted to do?**

   ▶ **Did Alex react cleverly?**

   ▶ **How else could Alex have reacted?**

3. ***Identify the Skill Components:*** List the following skill components on the board or sentence strips.

   1. Assess the situation.

   2. Identify the warning signs.

   3. Consider the consequences.

   4. Consider alternatives to involvement.

   5. React firmly but friendly.

91

4. ***Model the Skill:*** The teacher will role play a child, age 11, that is standing close to two teenagers who are talking about selling drugs to make some money. The teenagers suddenly see the child and assume that the child might have listened to what they discussed, therefore they shout at the child, "If you tell anybody what you heard, you will be sorry!" The teacher will use the skill components to show how they can guide the child to react cleverly.

5. ***Behavioral Rehearsal:***

   A. *Selection:* The teacher will select three students to role play.

   B. *Role Plays:* The teacher will give the students the following scenario to role play:

   – Three students are walking home and are talking about stopping at the drugstore and shoplifting some candy. One of the students makes the decision not to get involved.

   If time permits, the teacher will ask another three students to role play a similar scenario with the students considering "car jacking" instead of "shoplifting."

   C. *Completion:* After each role play, the teacher should reinforce the correct behavior and identify inappropriate behaviors, and ask the students to repeat the role play with corrections, if necessary. If it is done correctly, the role play is complete.

   D. *Reinforcers:* The class and teacher will applaud the role play. Verbal and non-verbal praise from both the teacher and the class is essential.

   E. *Discussion:* The teacher will lead the class in a discussion by asking the children to tell about similar situations they had actually experienced and how they reacted to them then and how they would react now, using the skills of this lesson. The teacher can also start a discussion by asking one of the children to write on the chalkboard warning signs and proper reactions to them which the teacher will ask the classmates to call out.

6. ***Practice:*** The teacher will ask the students to complete the worksheet "Trouble" and discuss it during class.

7. ***Independent Use:*** The teacher will distribute the worksheet "Danger" for students to complete as a homework assignment and return in one week for discussion in class.

8. ***Continuation:*** The teacher will tell the children that it is important for their own safety to learn the skills to spot trouble and have available a fast response and reaction to avoid danger and violence. These skills will help them not only during their young age but will be needed during their entire life since dangerous situations can occur momentarily at any time of their life.

Name _____ Date _____

TROUBLE

Directions: Complete the following paragraphs in the spaces below.

1. I am walking home from the playground which is two blocks away, thinking of the fun I had playing with my friends, when a car stops right next to me. I look up and see a man opening the door and saying "Would you like to have a little dog? I have her here in my car. She needs a home. I want to give you the dog if you like her and she likes you." I love dogs and have asked my mother many times to get one. I am tempted . . .

_____

_____

_____

_____

_____

_____

_____

_____

_____

_____

2. I am home alone. A stranger rings the doorbell. The stranger wants to use our phone. I . . .

_____

_____

_____

_____

_____

_____

_____

_____

_____

_____

Name _____ Date _____

DANGER

Directions: Describe an actual or invented violent situation from which you removed yourself because you detected a warning signal and decided to avoid the danger by not getting involved.

Situation: _____

_____

_____

_____

_____

_____

_____

_____

Answer and describe the following items:

1. What was the warning signal? _____

_____

2. What made you believe there was potential danger? _____

_____

3. What do you think could have happened to you if you got involved?

_____

4. How did you react? _____

_____

5. Describe your feelings when successful. _____

_____

6. Describe your feelings in case you could not succeed. _____

_____

Dealing with Dangerous Situations

Behavioral Objective: Students will learn to deal with potentially dangerous situations when they are confronted by one or involved in one.

Directed Lesson:

1. **Establish the Need:** Certain activities in the life of a young person can become dangerous or violent. Often, a split-second decision to either do or not do something can result in a life or death situation. Young people need to learn to think and act quickly to avoid violent situations which may be an outcome of rash judgment.

2. **Introduction:** The teacher will read the following story to the class:

"THE RED VETTE"

Jamie, age 10, had a friend, Aaron, who had just turned 16. He had just gotten his temporary driver's license. One nice Saturday Aaron's older brother, who was a college student, was not at home, and Aaron decided to show Jamie his older brother's red Vette. It was a high-speed car that had a big engine and looked like a racing car. It was capable of obtaining speeds of 120 miles per hour or more. Before long, Aaron had started it, pulled it out of the garage, and invited Jamie to take a "quick ride." Soon they were on the freeway doing 85 MPH—they passed the speed signs indicating a construction zone with a maximum speed of 45 MPH and double fines. They also passed a billboard that read, "Speed Kills." Then the sky became very dark, and it began to rain heavily. The road surface became wet and slippery. Aaron could feel the car sliding from side to side, but they were still traveling at a high speed.

The teacher will then call on students to complete the story. Each of the students' individual responses will be listed on the board. Then, the teacher will ask the following questions:

> ▶ **How could this be a dangerous situation?**
> ▶ **What are some questions Jamie should have asked himself before going along?**
> ▶ **What could or should Jamie now do?**

3. **Identify the Skill Components:** Write the following skill components on the board:

   1. Think ahead before getting involved.
   2. Consider the seriousness of the situation.
   3. React quickly but calmly, when you are in it.
   4. Consider steps needed to remain safe.
   5. Help the situation by using conversation.

6. Call for help.

7. Get away if possible.

8. Seek assistance.

4. *Model the Skill:* The teacher will model how to use the skill components by portraying the actions of a student who is approached by a person pointing a gun at him/her. The teacher will show how one may try to diffuse such a dangerous situation.

5. *Behavioral Rehearsal:*

    A. *Selection:* The teacher will select two pairs of students.

    B. *Role Plays:* The teacher will ask the first pair of students to role play the story in the lesson's Introduction and the second pair of students to play a story similar to the one the teacher used to model the skill.

    C. *Completion:* The teacher and the students' classmates will determine if the skill components were used properly. If so and there were no corrections, the role play is complete. If not, the teacher, with the assistance of the class, will identify the changes needed and ask the students to re-enact the role play.

    D. *Reinforcers:* The teacher will thank the participants and acknowledge the good work that was done.

    E. *Discussion:* Small groups of students within the class will be selected to discuss what they would have done in similar situations.

6. *Practice:* The teacher will have students complete the worksheet entitled "Danger Ahead." The students may read the completed story to the class to discuss it further.

7. *Independent Use:* The teacher will distribute the worksheet entitled "Safe Sailing" and ask the students to take it home and work on it with a parent. They are to return it in a prescribed period of time to discuss in class.

8. *Continuation:* Periodically, the teacher will ask the students to cut out articles from the newspaper which highlight how dangerous situations may be diffused. They may post these on the bulletin board or use them for classroom discussions.

Name _____ Date _____

DANGER AHEAD

Directions: Describe how you would solve the following 3 situations in a safe and peaceful manner. Use the skill components.

1. **Sally is playing with a friend in the basement and her friend takes a pack of matches out of her pocket. This is a new friend and she likes her a lot and does not want to lose her as a friend. She knows she is not supposed to play with matches.**

   _____

   _____

   _____

   _____

2. **Jack is going to a new school and he does not want to be considered a wimp. In his old school students teased him and he never was able to make friends easily. He is glad he is able to make a new start.**

   On his first day at the new school he meets Joe on the bus. Joe invites him to his house to play. In the house there is a gun on a shelf in the living room. Jack knows his mother wou'ld not want him to play in a house with a gun not locked up.

   _____

   _____

   _____

   _____

3. **While riding on the bus Sally sees Leslie take out a can opener, cut the bus seat cover with it, then quickly put the can opener back into her bookbag.**

   _____

   _____

   _____

   _____

Name _____ Date _____

SAFE SAILING

Directions: Write about three dangerous situations and how to handle them.

DANGEROUS SITUATION	WHAT IS THE SAFEST WAY TO HANDLE THIS SITUATION
1. _____ _____ _____	1. _____ _____ _____
2. _____ _____ _____	2. _____ _____ _____
3. _____ _____ _____	3. _____ _____ _____

_____
Parent Signature

Realizing Extreme Potential Danger

Behavioral Objective: Children will learn how to apply decision-making strategies to deal with potentially dangerous situations involving other individuals.

Directed Lesson:

1. **Establish the Need:** In today's society, young children are increasingly targets of strangers, whom they trust. As a result, they frequently become victims of violence or foul play. Youngsters need to understand the existence of such potential and to feel empowered to deal with dangerous situations.

2. **Introduction:** The teacher will ask the students the following questions in a general class discussion:

   ▶ **Have you ever witnessed a threatening situation in your neighborhood?**

   ▶ **If so, describe it. (Call upon individual students.)**

   Then, ask randomly selected children:

   ▶ **What would you do if someone offered to give you a ride?**

   ▶ **What would you do if someone offered you a drink from an opened container?**

   ▶ **What would you do if someone offered you an unwrapped candy?**

   ▶ **Describe a "stranger." What makes this person strange? How would you react to this stranger?**

   The teacher will read the following scenario to the class:

   John and Brandy were brother and sister, ages 6 and 8 respectively. One day on the way home from school, they were lagging behind other students who were walking home from school. They were walking slowly, dragging their bookbags on the ground.

   Then a man named Charlie pulled up in his big black Buick alongside of them and asked Brandy to "return to school with him" to pick up something that her mother had called him about. Charlie was known as a "loner" and an alcoholic to many in the neighborhood. Once Brandy had even seen him drinking a large 40-ounce bottle of beer on his front porch.

   Charlie said he was in a hurry; that they would pick up the things at the school and that John could continue on home. Brandy told her brother to "run along" and that she would see him later.

   The teacher will ask the following questions:

   ▶ **What would you have done?**

99

> ◗ **Was it dangerous for Brandy to go with Charlie?**
> ◗ **Should Brandy have continued to walk home?**
> ◗ **What did Brandy know about Charlie?**

3. ***Identify the Skill Components:*** Write the following skill components on the board.

   1. Consider carefully the entire situation.

   2. Determine if you could be in danger.

   3. Recognize possible danger.

   4. Think carefully how to act.

   5. Determine how to get out of the situation.

   6. Scream and run if necessary.

   7. Seek help.

4. ***Model the Skill:*** The teacher will describe how he/she left the school after a late evening open house program for his/her car which was parked in a far corner of the dark parking lot. As the teacher approached the car, he/she sighted a dark car on the other side of the fence. Two males were sitting in this car talking in loud voices and drinking, what seemed to be beer, from bottles. They were both staring at his/her car.

   Using a "think aloud" approach, the teacher will show how the skill components could be used to help in avoiding danger.

5. ***Behavioral Rehearsal:***

   A. *Selection:* The teacher will select three pairs of students to role play.

   B. *Role Plays:* The teacher will ask each pair of students to play one of the following scenarios and use the skill components.

      – A "friend" invites you to his home to "show you something." When you arrive and talk, he asks you to come to his father's bedroom where his dad keeps a loaded "22."

      – While you are home, awaiting the arrival of your mother, a man (stranger) comes to the front door, rings the bell and wants to come in to give you something for your mom.

      – As you leave school alone, a lady pulls up in a red "flashy car," and calls to you, asking who you are, and where you live. She then indicates that she notices that you are carrying many school books. Then she tells you that she lives "up the street from you" and offers you a ride home.

   C. *Completion:* After each group role plays, reinforce correct comments and behavior, identify inappropriate comments and behavior, and if necessary have the students repeat the role play with corrections. If there are no corrections, role play is complete.

   D. *Reinforcers:* The teacher and class will acknowledge the performance of the participants by giving applause and praise to all role players.

   E. *Discussion:* The teacher will discuss with the class how to use the skill components when confronted with a dangerous situation and will start the discussion by posing the following questions:

> ▶ **If you find yourself in a dangerous situation, how do you think you would deal with it? Would the skill components help you in deciding how to act?**

6. ***Practice:*** The teacher will distribute copies of the worksheet "Stranger/Danger" to students, ask them to complete it, then discuss the students' responses.

7. ***Independent Use:*** Distribute copies of the "Threats to Me" worksheet to the students, with instructions to complete it at home. The completed worksheet should be returned at a specified time for class discussion.

8. ***Continuation:*** The teacher will routinely reinforce learnings about threatening situations and how to respond to strangers. A periodic send-home sheet of recommended actions in dealing with strangers would be appropriate for children and parents.

Name _____ Date _____

STRANGER/DANGER

Directions: Write what you would do when confronted with the following situations:

SITUATION	WHAT WILL YOU DO?
1. **Unwanted/unknown visitor**	1. _____
	_____
2. **Free ride in car**	2. _____
	_____
3. **Candy or other substance**	3. _____
	_____
4. **Threatening phone call**	4. _____
	_____

LIST OTHER SUCH SITUATIONS	WHAT WILL YOU DO?
1. _____	1. _____
	_____
2. _____	2. _____
	_____
3. _____	3. _____
	_____
4. _____	4. _____
	_____

Name _____ Date _____

THREATS to ME

Directions: Describe what you consider is most frightening and what you would do if it should happen and try to discuss it with your parent(s).

SITUATIONS AND THINGS THAT FRIGHTEN ME MOST	WHAT DO I DO IN RESPONSE TO THESE?
1. _____	1. _____
2. _____	2. _____
3. _____	3. _____
4. _____	4. _____
5. _____	5. _____
6. _____	6. _____
7. _____	7. _____

What have I learned from this lesson which would help me most?

_____

_____

Did you discuss these situations with your parent(s)? Yes _____ No _____

If yes, ask parent to sign.

_____

Parent

Learning to Trust Others

Behavioral Objective: Students will learn to gain trust in others and, thus, be able to communicate with others when difficulties arise.

Directed Lesson:

1. **Establish the Need:** Young children need to learn how to build trust in others. While building trust, they will gain a sense of confidence and will be better able to seek help in their early lives. Seeking such help will enable them to avoid frustrations, self doubt, and feelings of insecurity.

2. **Introduction:** The teacher will relate the following story to the students:

> **John is a talented high school senior who is also a member of the Big Brothers organization. Big Brothers is a community organization that pairs older boys with younger ones, and the older boys serve as "big brothers" or role models to the younger boys. Jimmy is a bright and likeable boy who is a kindergarten student. His father recently passed away, and his dad was someone in whom he could always confide and a person who demonstrated self-confidence, was hard working and, above all, was true to his word. Soon after his dad's death Jimmy began to have trouble in school. Often he was so sad that he thought of dying or even "ending it all." He, with the advice of his mom, began to spend more time with John. On the weekends John would often take him to the ballgame, and they soon began to enjoy each other's company.**

The teacher then asks the following questions:

> ❿ **How has Jim come to such a point and so upset that everything seemed to be insurmountable?**
>
> ❿ **How can this situation be resolved without harm to Jim?**
>
> ❿ **Would it help Jim to have someone in whom he can confide and why?**
>
> ❿ **Is there someone Jim can trust? Who might it be?**
>
> ❿ **What characteristics should a person have in whom you can trust?**

3. **Identify the Skill Components:** Write the following skill components on the board:

   1. Identify the characteristics a person of trust should have.

   2. Select someone who is similar to another person you respect.

   3. Communicate with that person and share your concerns.

   4. Listen carefully to what is being said.

   5. Use the information to help resolve the problem.

104

4. ***Model the Skill:*** Using the story from the introduction, the teacher will portray Jimmy and role play how the skill components could improve the situation. Another student may be selected to role play John.

5. ***Behavioral Rehearsal:***

A. *Selection:* The teacher will select three pairs of students to role play.

B. *Role Plays:* One student in each of the pairs selected will role play the person in trouble, and the other will portray the trusted person. The following are suggested role play topics:

- Pressure by a parent to do well in school.

- A student who is new to the community and is having difficulty making new friends.

- A young person who learns first-hand and for the first time of a parent's serious and terminal illness.

C. *Completion:* The class will evaluate each of the role plays and also how well the skill components were applied in the role play. If there are no corrections, the role play is complete. If there are corrections, the students will redo the role play.

D. *Reinforcers:* The teacher will acknowledge each student who participated for their ideas in solving difficult situations and give praise.

E. *Discussion:* The teacher will ask the following questions:

▶ **How can talking with a person you trust help to solve a troubling situation?**

▶ **Why is thinking about hurting oneself one of the worst possible choices to make?**

▶ **If you knew a person who was troubled, what are some things you could do to help?**

▶ **Is there anyone who would be able to share with the class an example of "when they needed to 'talk out' a situation with a trusting person," and could describe how that person assisted in solving the problem.**

6. ***Practice:*** The teacher will distribute the worksheet entitled "Who Can I Trust?" for students to complete and follow up with discussion.

Note: Primary students can draw a picture of a person whom they trust, then show the picture to the class and tell why.

7. ***Independent Use:*** The teacher will ask the students to complete the worksheet entitled "Why I Do Not Trust You" to return to class within one week.

8. ***Continuation:*** The teacher will emphasize routinely that during our entire lives each of us sometimes needs someone to turn to, namely a person to be trusted.

Name _____ Date _____

Who Can I Trust?

Directions: List below the important characteristics of a person you *do* or can trust. Be able to tell the class why each characteristic is important.

1. _____
2. _____
3. _____
4. _____
5. _____
6. _____
7. _____
8. _____

Directions: Name a person(s) who you trust most. Tell why you trust him or her.

Who? _____

Why? _____

_____

_____

_____

_____

_____

_____

_____

_____

_____

_____

_____

_____

Name _____   Date _____

Why I Do Not Trust You . . .

Directions: Draw a picture of someone you do not trust—then tell why. Fill in the face and dress of the stick person.

WHY?

_____

_____

_____

_____

_____

_____

_____

_____

_____

Learning to Manage Excessive Stress

Behavioral Objective: Students will learn how to manage and limit excessive stress that might be self-imposed or that might be caused by pressure from others.

Directed Lesson:

1. **Establish the Need:** Some students are very ambitious in wanting to excel in all undertakings, even if it is extremely difficult. Also frequently parents and friends will pressure youngsters to become achievers even in fields that children know that they have little ability to master. The adults, although meaning well, do not realize that the amount of pressure exerted on the growing children can produce excessive stress which can do great harm and can lead to violent outbreaks, depression and even suicide. The children will learn to understand that the adults mean well and that they themselves have to judge how much they are able to achieve. Following the judgment, the children have to learn to limit their activities in order to keep their stress at a manageable level. They have also to understand that self-imposed stress is equally dangerous when in excess.

2. **Introduction:** The teacher will read the following story to the class:

   Marty was elected captain of the junior swimming team. This was a real honor for him because there were several other boys who swam just as well as him, but he was chosen to lead the team. He enjoyed the other boys and they liked him. Now that he was the captain, however, he felt that he had to swim even better. Marty started to get up early to exercise and really work out. He would go to the pool early just to be there when the doors opened. He ran after swimming thinking this would build up his speed in the pool. When the team lost he was so upset he would cry at night before he fell asleep. He started to lose weight and became very nervous. When the boys asked him to play or just hang out he would say no because he did not enjoy being with other people as much as previously. He just worried about the team and if it would win the next time around. This hope kept him going.

   The teacher could lead the discussion with the following questions:

   ▶ **Who is putting pressure on Marty?**

   ▶ **How do you know Marty is stressed out?**

   ▶ **Why do you think Marty is putting this pressure on himself?**

   ▶ **Who can Marty go to for help?**

   ▶ **How can someone help Marty?**

3. **Identify the Skill Components:** Write the following skill components on the board or on sentence strips:

108

1. Determine your stress level.
2. Decide who exerts the pressure.
3. Analyze the danger resulting from the excessive stress.
4. Decide how much stress you can manage.
5. Discuss your limitations with those responsible for the excessive stress.
6. Make a plan to adjust your activities to achieve a manageable stress level.
7. Ask for help, if needed.
8. Follow through with your plan.

4. **Model the Skill:** The teacher will relate a real or imagined story about a student who was pressured into getting A's, although the student did not have the ability to achieve such a grade. The teacher will use the skill components to show how the student successfully solved his problem and managed the stress exerted on him.

5. **Behavioral Rehearsal:**

   A. *Selection:* The teacher will select two pairs of students.

   B. *Role Plays:* Two students will use the story in the lesson's introduction as a basis for their role play. One student will be Marty and the other a student on the swim team. The student on the swim team can respond to Marty as he sees fit.

   The second pair of students will role play a brother and sister who, while their mother is in jail, must live with their grandmother who puts excessive stress on them by . . .

   C. *Completion:* After each role play, the teacher and class will decide if the role play was done correctly. If not, the teacher will ask the students to re-do the role play. If there are no corrections, the role play is complete.

   D. *Reinforcers:* The teacher thanks the students for their role playing and the class will give praise and applaud.

   E. *Discussion:* The teacher can start a discussion by asking the following questions:

   ▶ **How do you cope with stressful situations?**

   ▶ **Explain how you can use the skill components to help in a stressful situation?**

   ▶ **Why must we learn to cope with excessive stress?**

   ▶ **Is excessive stress dangerous?**

   ▶ **Can excessive stress lead to violence? Why?**

6. **Practice:** The teacher will distribute the worksheet "Excessive Stress" and ask the students to answer the questions and to discuss their answers in class.

7. **Independent Use:** The teacher will distribute the worksheet "Stress in a Box" for the students to do at home and ask them to return it completed in one week for discussion in class.

8. **Continuation:** The teacher will indicate that all through life people are confronted with situations that exert excessive stress. Therefore, it is important for everyone to understand his/her manageable stress level and to know how to control activities accordingly in order to limit stress. The teacher will emphasize that stress, which is in excess of being manageable, can lead to depression and violent behavior and ultimately may destroy healthy lifestyles.

Name _____ Date _____

EXCESSIVE STRESS

Directions: Answer the following questions:

1. Why is it necessary to learn to limit excessive stress and to understand your limitation? (Use the skill components.)

   _____

   _____

2. What do you consider is the stress level you can manage?

   _____

3. How do you manage to keep your stress below or at this level?

   _____

   _____

4. Is it best to operate under stress that is close to your manageable stress level?

   _____

5. How can you adjust your stress?

   _____

   _____

6. How do you increase stress?

   _____

7. How do you decrease stress?

   _____

8. Can you regulate the amount of stress which is best for you? How?

   _____

   _____

   _____

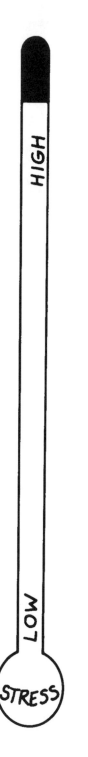

Name _____ Date _____

STRESS IN A BOX

Directions: Talk with your parents. Share the skill components for managing excessive stress with them. Ask them if they would use the same or similar skills to cope with an extremely stressful situation of their own.

    Then write a story or draw a picture about something that could happen to you which would put excessive stress on you and tell how you would go about limiting your stress to manageable proportions.

My Story

_____
_____
_____
_____
_____
_____
_____
_____
_____
_____
_____
_____
_____
_____
_____

Coping with Extreme Stress

Behavioral Objective: Students will learn skills to help them cope with extreme stressful situations, such as neglect, divorce, parental fights, death in the family and others.

Directed Lesson:

1. ***Establish the Need:*** In today's society youngsters are bombarded by stress-producing events, such as crime, loss of a family member, parental disagreements, divorce of parents, accidents, fights, accusations, neglect, rejection, hatred and others, which have become more frequent, or at least it appears so because of better and faster transmission of information. These events take on unbelievable proportions in children's minds and the excessive stress can produce trauma and self-accusations and can lead to violence, injury, death and self-destruction. Children will learn skills that can help them to cope with such situations.

2. ***Introduction:*** The teacher will read the following story:

   Peter, eight years old, just lost his grandfather who had lived with him, his mother and his older sister as long as he can remember. His grandfather was like a father to him. He respected him and followed his advice. He was the only man in the family and the only man he ever loved and admired. He never knew his father who had left his mother shortly after he was born. Peter, being deeply attached to his grandfather and depending on him for counsel, was completely lost when he learned about his sudden death. He felt he had nobody left who cared for him. His mother, working all day and coming home late and tired, frequently got angry with him for not having done this or that but never, as he thought, with his sister. This made him feel rejected and the idea crossed his mind that all would be better if he were not around. This idea grew while days passed, and he wondered how best to end his life or disappear from his mother's house.

   The teacher will ask the following questions:

   ◗ **Do you think that Peter was rejected?**
   ◗ **Was Peter overly sensitive due to stress?**
   ◗ **What do you think of Peter's idea to leave his mother or commit suicide?**
   ◗ **What would you suggest for Peter to do?**

3. ***Identify the Skill Components:*** Write the following skill components on the board or on sentence strips:

   1. Decide if the imposed stress is excessive or tolerable.

   2. Determine the stress level that you can tolerate.

3. Identify ways to decrease the stress to your own tolerance level.

4. Analyze if the stress is self-inflicted or imposed by others.

5. Consider constructive actions needed to decrease, minimize or ignore the stress.

6. Analyze the consequences of those actions.

7. Decide if you need help.

8. If yes, select a trustworthy adult.

9. Make a rational decision.

4. ***Model the Skill:*** The teacher will role play Peter from the story in the lesson's introduction and show by using the skill components how Peter can cope with the event in a rational and constructive manner.

5. ***Behavioral Rehearsal:***

   A. *Selection:* The teacher will select five groups of students of appropriate number to role play.

   B. *Role Plays:* Each group of students will role play one of the scenarios similar to those below. The teacher might want to give more detailed instructions to the students.
      - Heated argument at home.
      - Seeing the family pet mistreated and ignored.
      - Fight on the street.
      - Induced by promises to accompany a stranger.
      - Witnessing an assault or a threat with a gun, on a family member.

   C. *Completion:* After each role play, the teacher will decide if the role play was done correctly. If corrections are needed, the role play will be re-enacted; if not, the role play is complete.

   D. *Reinforcers:* The teacher and class will thank the role players for their participation with applause and verbal compliments.

   E. *Discussion:* The teacher will start the discussion by asking the class to name excessive stressful events and having one student list them on the board. This can lead to a discussion about the skill components and how they can help to cope with those events in a rational and peaceful manner.

6. ***Practice:*** The teacher will distribute the worksheet "Stress and Me" for completion in class, after which there will be a general discussion.

7. ***Independent Use:*** The teacher will ask the students to complete the worksheet entitled "Overcoming My Stress" at home and return it within one week for a class discussion.

8. ***Continuation:*** The teacher will regularly remind students that everyone experiences stressful situations in life and how important it is to respond to these stressful situations in a calm and reasonable manner.

Name _____ Date _____

STRESS AND ME

Directions: On the lines below, list four situations that cause you the greatest stress.

1. _____

   _____

2. _____

   _____

3. _____

   _____

4. _____

   _____

Directions: Now tell how you cope with each of these stressful situations.

1. _____

   _____

2. _____

   _____

3. _____

   _____

4. _____

   _____

Name _____ Date _____

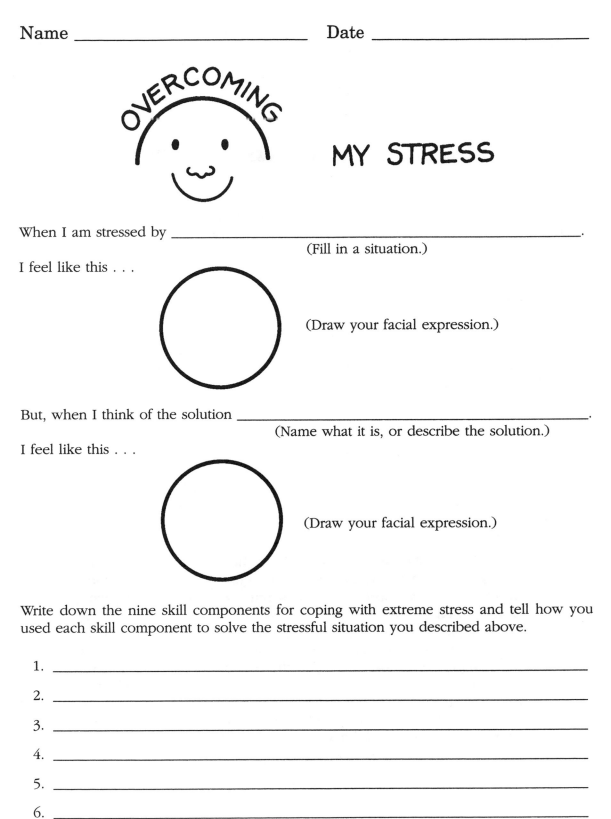

When I am stressed by _____.
(Fill in a situation.)

I feel like this . . .

(Draw your facial expression.)

But, when I think of the solution _____.
(Name what it is, or describe the solution.)

I feel like this . . .

(Draw your facial expression.)

Write down the nine skill components for coping with extreme stress and tell how you used each skill component to solve the stressful situation you described above.

1. _____
2. _____
3. _____
4. _____
5. _____
6. _____
7. _____
8. _____
9. _____

Dealing with Loneliness and Depression

Behavioral Objective: Students have to learn that if they are feeling lonely or depressed, they should look for an adult to help them and that help is available if they ask for it.

Directed Lesson:

1. ***Establish the Need:*** Suicide among teenagers is common and unfortunately it is being considered by children of younger and younger age. A lonely and depressed child even at a very young age has ideas of suicide in mind since suicide is mentioned on television, especially during the news broadcasts and thus has become common knowledge. Children frequently do not realize that death ends everything for them and thus fear in life is a greater threat than fear of death. Loneliness and depression might be due to sickness, neglect by parent(s), harassment and rejection by peers, dislike for the teacher, failure in school, abuse at home and a multitude of other reasons. Usually a child considering suicide will not discuss his/her problems with anybody and if asked, will not be able to convey in words the reasons for his/her destructive thoughts since the child really does not know what causes those feelings. Children have to understand that life should and can be full of good feelings and joy, especially if they share with others their happy and sad feelings and that life is there to live fully and not to be destroyed.

2. ***Introduction:*** The teacher will read the following story:

   Jimmy liked to play with other children, but he never felt like he belonged. He started spending more and more time playing alone. It just seemed like too much of an effort to be around others. He started to daydream frequently, but his daydreams turned into thoughts of loneliness and hopelessness. Nothing seemed to get a smile, let alone a laugh, out of Jimmy. Everything went from bad to worse. Even when his mother made his favorite cake, he was not hungry. His cousins were going to come over and even the thought of it made him more depressed. At night he would just flop in bed. He stopped brushing his teeth and bathing before bed. He just did not feel like doing it. Life was getting too hard to cope with and he thought it might be better if he just ended his life. He heard of people doing this on TV and maybe that is what he should do.

   The teacher will ask the following question and list the answers on the chalkboard:

   ▶ **Why do you think Jimmy felt this way?**

3. ***Identify the Skill Components:*** Write the following skill components on the board or on sentence strips:

   1. Think about the reasons for feeling lonely and depressed.

   2. Think of the consequences if you give in to those feelings.

116

3. Decide if the cause is you or others.

4. Decide to do whatever is necessary (change, forgive) to regain your interest in life.

5. Think about how happy and joyful life can be.

6. Consider interesting activities that might help.

7. Consider sharing your problems.

8. Consider a constructive solution.

4. **Model the Skill:** The teacher will portray a child who feels like Jimmy in the story of the lesson's introduction and talk the class through the skill components in detail to illustrate how they should be used by the children themselves to remedy and solve constructively, situations similar to the one experienced by Jimmy.

5. **Behavioral Rehearsal:**

A. *Selection:* The teacher will select four students to role play.

B. *Role Plays:* The teacher will ask each student to select one reason or more from the answers to the question in the introduction, which are still on the chalkboard, and to show how a student can use the skill components to arrive at a constructive solution after he/she recognizes the reasons for his/her feelings of sadness and/or depression and finds a way to regain his/her interest in life.

C. *Completion:* After each role play, the teacher will decide if the role play was done correctly and if the skill components were used appropriately. If corrections are needed, the role play will be re-enacted; if not, the role play is complete.

D. *Reinforcers:* The teacher and class will thank the role players for their performance with applause and verbal compliments.

E. *Discussion:* The teacher will start the discussion by asking the children the following questions:

▶ **How do you recognize if any of your friends or peers are depressed?**

▶ **How can you help them?**

▶ **Did any of you ever feel like Jimmy?**

▶ **If you get depressed, would you try to get out of such feelings? How?**

6. **Practice:** The teacher will distribute copies of the worksheet "Feelings of Depression— What?—Who?" for students to complete and discuss in class.

7. **Independent Use:** The teacher will distribute copies of the worksheet "Over the Top" to take home and return completed in one week for discussion in class.

8. **Continuation:** The teacher will emphasize how wonderful life can be and that all problems in life can be solved in a constructive and positive manner. There is never any need to give up in despair.

Name _____ Date _____

FEELINGS OF DEPRESSION
WHAT—WHO?

Directions: Answer the following questions in complete sentences.

A. What are behaviors or attitudes of someone who is depressed?

    1. _____

    2. _____

    3. _____

B. What can a person do to help him/herself when depressed?

    1. _____

    2. _____

    3. _____

C. What can someone else do to help a depressed person?

    1. _____

    2. _____

    3. _____

Write down the skill components.

    1. _____

    2. _____

    3. _____

    4. _____

    5. _____

    6. _____

    7. _____

    8. _____

Name _____ Date _____

OVER THE TOP

Directions: Write a paragraph about each of the following and use the skill components to help you. Share your work with your parent(s).

1. Describe a situation or make up one where someone felt "overwhelmed" by depression and loneliness.

_____

_____

_____

_____

2. Interview your parent(s) and write about a time when he/she was depressed.

_____

_____

_____

_____

3. What did he/she do to improve his/her feelings?

_____

_____

_____

_____

4. What would you do in a similar situation?

_____

_____

_____

_____

_____

Learning About Developing Bad Habits

Behavioral Objective: Students will learn that repeated actions and behaviors can lead to developing addictions to bad habits that are difficult to change, once established, and that some of these addictions, such as the use of stimulants, can be formed after a first try.

Directed Lesson:

1. **Establish the Need:** Youngsters usually do not realize how easily bad habits are formed and grow to become addictions. Bad habits, such as cursing, fighting, bullying, bad mouthing and others, when repeatedly used, can become second nature in no time, and the use of stimulants might cause addictions even after a first try. It is important for youngsters to learn that bad habits are mostly antisocial and unlawful and could cause violence and result in great harm to themselves and others. Therefore, children should learn to avoid developing bad habits and bad behavior by knowing the facts about addiction and how difficult it is to lose any bad habit once acquired.

2. **Introduction:** The teacher will ask the students to identify some bad habits and list them on the board. The teacher will then explain that many bad habits are addictive and often it is very difficult to get rid of those addictions. The teacher will then read the following story:

   Susie is a 9-year-old girl and has many friends in school and outside of school. Susie and some of her friends have been seen using tobacco, some have become regular smokers, and some have begun to use other stimulants—and some have even sniffed glue. Among these stimulants are also drugs that are used for health reasons or others requiring a doctor's prescription. Some of these drugs made them feel happy, others have made them sad, and some have made them feel real relaxed. Susie and her friends have found that their craving for these stimulants becomes more and more frequent.

   The teacher will ask the students the following questions.

   ▶ **Was Susie addicted?**
   ▶ **What was the cause of Susie's addiction?**
   ▶ **What asocial activities have you done many times? How did you feel about it at first?**
   ▶ **Did it feel easier to repeat the activity?**
   ▶ **Who could help Susie address her problem?**
   ▶ **How do you think she feels about her habit?**
   ▶ **How do her friends feel?**
   ▶ **Will there be lasting effects of these habits? What are they?**

3. **Identify the Skill Components:** Write the following skill components on the board:

   1. Understand that most bad habits including the use of stimulants are addictive.

120

2. Consider the consequences of forming bad habits.

3. Remember that often one try can lead to a bad habit and addiction.

4. If already addicted, understand that you may need help.

5. Value your life.

6. Make a wise decision.

4. *Model the Skill:* The teacher will role play a student who had smoked marijuana for the first time. The teacher will then demonstrate how the use of the skill components could help in making a rational and wise decision, namely to avoid another smoke.

5. *Behavioral Rehearsal:*

   A. *Selection:* The teacher will select two groups of three students each to role play the following role plays.

   B. *Role Plays:*
      (1) Use of illegal drugs;
      (2) swearing;
      (3) stealing.

   C. *Completion:* The teacher will discuss with the class each role play and determine whether the skill components were used appropriately. If not, the teacher will ask the students to repeat the role play with correction. If yes, the role play is completed.

   D. *Reinforcers:* The teacher will acknowledge the participation of the students in the role play with great praise.

   E. *Discussion:* The teacher will ask the following questions to spark a class discussion:

   ▶ **What are the symptoms of the formation of bad habits?**
   ▶ **Why do bad habits affect each of us in different ways?**
   ▶ **Can you determine before developing a bad habit how it will affect you?**
   ▶ **What is the best way to avoid developing bad habits?**
   ▶ **How can the use of the skill components assist you in avoiding the development of bad habits?**

6. *Practice:* The teacher will distribute copies of the worksheet entitled "Habits And Me" for completion in class. The students will then be asked to share responses with the class.

7. *Independent Use:* The teacher will distribute the worksheet "Habit Poster" and ask students to develop posters at home, which warn about the development of specific bad habits, and return them to class in one week for discussion.

8. *Continuation:* The teacher will use the posters that the students have returned on a periodic basis as motivation for them to avoid developing bad habits.

Name _____ Date _____

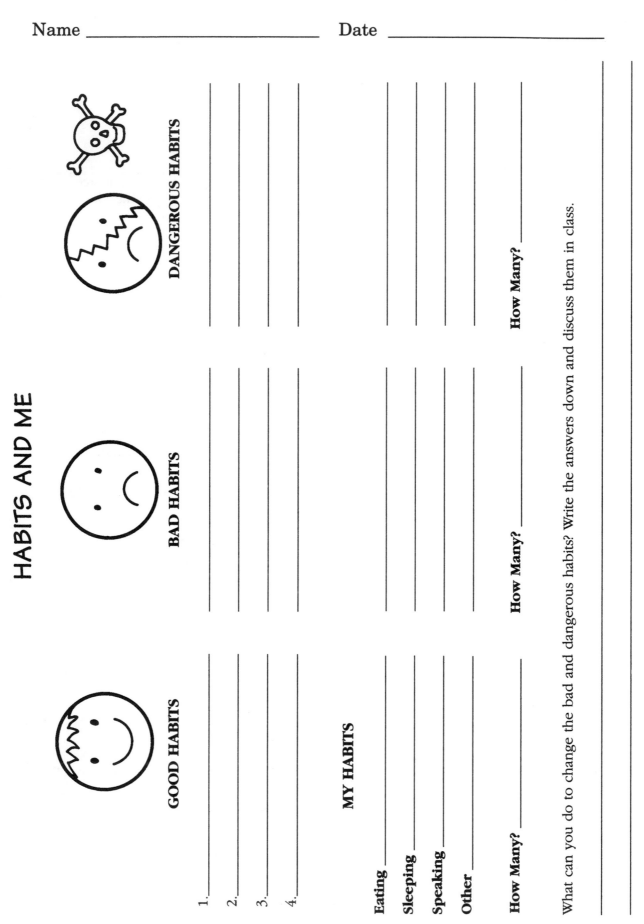

HABITS AND ME

GOOD HABITS

1. _____
2. _____
3. _____
4. _____

BAD HABITS

_____
_____
_____
_____

DANGEROUS HABITS

_____
_____
_____
_____

MY HABITS

Eating _____
Sleeping _____
Speaking _____
Other _____

How Many? _____   **How Many?** _____   **How Many?** _____

What can you do to change the bad and dangerous habits? Write the answers down and discuss them in class.

_____

Name _____ Date _____

HABIT POSTER

Directions: Draw a poster which sends a message about the dangers of forming bad habits.

Understanding the Effects of Stimulant Use

Behavioral Objective: Children will learn to recognize the harmful physical and mental effects stimulants can have and will understand that stimulant use by minors is illegal.

Directed Lesson:

1. **Establish the Need:** Children know, even at a very young age, that certain stimulants, such as alcohol, are used by adults to feel good, celebrate special occasions, and give the appearance of being happy. Children often experiment with stimulants because of their strong desire to imitate their adult role models and to enjoy the same pleasure they observe in these role models. Children need to realize that stimulants do not always create euphoric feelings, but can cause people to become sick, mean, argumentative, irresponsible, and even violent. Also stimulants can be addictive and are harmful to a person's health. Their use is illegal for minors. Understanding all these facts and their consequences, children will become very careful to avoid experimenting with stimulants even when tempted by others to participate in their folly.

2. **Introduction:** The teacher will read the following story to the class:

   Mary, Susan, Bill and Joe, ranging from 7 to 10 years of age, were at a family party celebrating the 25th wedding anniversary of their Aunt Betty and Uncle Ken. As the party progressed, the children noticed how much the adults were smoking and drinking beer, wine and other types of alcohol. They noticed that some of the adults were elated, talked loudly and laughed a lot, some began to have trouble walking, missed the ashtrays and burned the table tops, and some even became rowdy and aggressive toward others. All of a sudden, Uncle Louie and a family friend, Frank, got very mad at each other, started shouting and then started to fight.

   Mary, Susan, Bill and Joe looked at each other and just shook their heads while observing the adults' behavior.

   The teacher will ask the following questions:

   ▸ **Why do you think adults indulged in the use of stimulants at the party?**
   ▸ **How do stimulants change a person's behavior?**
   ▸ **Why do you think Mary, Susan, Bill and Joe shook their heads while watching the fight?**
   ▸ **What is your personal opinion of stimulant use?**

3. ***Identify the Skill Components:*** The teacher will list the skill components on a chart or the chalkboard.

   1. Think about which substances are stimulants.

   2. Consider how stimulants can change behavior.

   3. Consider other consequences of stimulant use.

   4. Identify reasons for using stimulants.

   5. Decide if the reasons given represent excuses for you.

   6. Think of other activities to create good feelings.

   7. Act in your best interest.

4. ***Model the Skill:*** The teacher will role play an eight-year-old who is offered a drink of beer by a family friend; a student will play the part of the family friend. The skill components will guide the teacher to make a decision.

5. ***Behavioral Rehearsal:***

   A. *Selection:* For the first role play, the teacher will select 10 to 12 children and for the second role play the teacher will ask one child to do the role play.

   B. *Role Plays:*

   – Ten to twelve students will role play the introductory story.

   – A 10-year-old boy, Glenn, is cleaning the family room the morning after his parents had several couples at their home for a party. Glenn notices that some of the glasses still contain some liquor. He smells the liquor and wonders how it tastes.

   C. *Completion:* After each role play, the teacher and class will determine if the role play was done correctly. If not, the teacher will ask the students to re-enact the role play with the appropriate skills. If yes, the role play is complete.

   D. *Reinforcers:* The teacher and others in class will applaud the role playing students to show appreciation for their cooperation and participation and for having done well.

   E. *Discussion:* The teacher will start the discussion by asking the students what they have learned from the introductory story and role plays; and, how they arrived at a decision about stimulant use and what they think would be their decision.

6. ***Practice:*** The teacher will have the children complete the "Search for Facts" word search, giving assistance as needed, and then sharing answers.

7. ***Independent Use:*** The teacher will ask the students to draw a poster at home, about 18″ × 24″ in size, with a slogan about avoiding stimulants such as alcohol, and to bring it to class in one week. After displaying the posters in the classroom, the principal, a teacher or parent will select the five best posters to be placed in the hallways, and one student selected by the class, will be awarded a small prize for the best poster.

8. ***Continuation:*** The teacher will remind the children that it is important to know the facts and effects of stimulants such as alcohol. They should understand the dangerous effects stimulants have on the mind, emotions, behavior and health and that, depending on a person's age, some stimulants' use is illegal for minors and some stimulants are illegal, regardless of age. Children should be encouraged to make decisions based on facts and what is best for their future, which means avoiding the use of stimulants.

Name _____ Date _____

SEARCH FOR FACTS

A	R	G	U	M	E	N	T	I	V	E	A	B
D	O	C	D	E	S	F	G	H	I	J	H	K
D	W	L	M	N	T	O	P	O	R	S	A	T
I	D	U	V	W	I	X	Y	Z	A	C	R	E
C	Y	F	H	J	M	E	A	N	L	N	M	O
T	O	S	U	W	U	Y	C	E	G	I	F	K
I	M	O	R	T	L	V	X	Z	D	X	U	O
V	U	D	V	E	A	L	C	O	H	O	L	W
E	A	F	W	D	N	V	G	A	E	T	I	B
B	R	E	J	F	T	U	K	H	A	S	O	L
O	I	E	O	V	S	D	N	Z	L	M	A	Q
C	D	F	X	K	U	C	J	R	T	X	B	P
P	Y	W	L	T	O	H	S	G	H	M	Y	N
I	R	R	E	S	P	O	N	S	I	B	L	E

Directions: When you find these words, draw a line around them.

MEAN	**ADDICTIVE**	**IRRESPONSIBLE**
HARMFUL	**HEALTH**	**STIMULANTS**
ROWDY	**ARGUMENT**	**ALCOHOL**

Name _____ Date _____

SEARCH FOR FACTS

Answer Key

A	R	G	U	M	E	N	T	I	V	E	A	B
D	O	C	D	E	S	F	G	H	I	J	H	K
D	W	L	M	N	T	O	P	O	R	S	A	T
I	D	U	V	W	I	X	Y	Z	A	C	R	E
C	Y	F	H	J	M	E	A	N	L	N	M	O
T	O	S	U	W	U	Y	C	E	G	I	F	K
I	M	O	R	T	L	V	X	Z	D	X	U	O
V	U	D	V	E	A	L	C	O	H	O	L	W
E	A	F	W	D	N	V	G	A	E	T	I	B
B	R	E	J	F	T	U	K	H	A	S	O	L
O	I	E	O	V	S	D	N	Z	L	M	A	Q
C	D	F	X	K	U	C	J	R	T	X	B	P
P	Y	W	L	T	O	H	S	G	H	M	Y	N
I	R	R	E	S	P	O	N	S	I	B	L	E

Directions: When you find these words, draw a line around them.

MEAN	ADDICTIVE	IRRESPONSIBLE
HARMFUL	HEALTH	STIMULANTS
ROWDY	ARGUMENT	ALCOHOL

Understanding the Dangers of Marijuana

Behavioral Objective: Children will learn that marijuana is one of many dangerous stimulants which are highly addictive and are harmful to the body and mind.

Directed Lesson:

1. **Establish the Need:** Some children may believe that marijuana is a safe stimulant because it is a "natural product." First exposure usually occurs for reasons of experimentation and to belong to a group of students who urge the use of marijuana to "get high." Children need to understand the highly addictive quality of marijuana which can cause addiction on the first try. They must also learn that marijuana is an illegal drug and opens the door to experimentation with other, more dangerous drugs. By knowing the facts and consequences of using marijuana, the students will become aware of the serious problems they face when experimenting with any drug.

2. **Introduction:** The teacher will use the following story to introduce the skill:

   Danna liked her new elementary school, even though the kids did not seem as grown-up as the kids at her other school. At her old school, they had less parental supervision, therefore they had the freedom to do just about what they wanted to do including smoking marijuana at the park, at sleepovers, etc. Danna missed smoking marijuana with her old friends and thought she would introduce some of her new friends to marijuana. She started with Jane by inviting Jane to her home on Saturday when she knew her parents would not be home.

   Jane was not sure she wanted to try smoking "a joint" (marijuana); she had learned at school that it was an illegal drug and could be addictive. But Danna kept urging her and she thought about how smart and popular Danna was and that one try probably wouldn't hurt her. Soon she was puffing on a joint. She felt dizzy and felt like she might throw up. This is not what she expected and she did not like it. Danna urged her to continue a little longer. Before long, she and Danna were giggling and laughing at each other.

   The following questions can be used after the story:

   ◗ **Why did Jane decide to smoke the marijuana?**

   ◗ **What consequences will Jane have to face?**

   ◗ **What could Jane have done differently to make Danna want her as a friend but not get involved with drugs?**

3. **Identify the Skill Components:** The teacher will write the following skill components on a chart or the chalkboard.

1. Learn the facts and consequences about stimulants.

2. Remember that marijuana is as addictive as other stimulants.

3. Consider what harm marijuana will do to body and mind.

4. Think about possible responses when offered a stimulant.

5. Consider alternative activities.

6. Decide what is best for you.

4. *Model the Skill:* The teacher will model a student who is offered marijuana by a member of a popular group at school and is tempted to smoke it in order to be accepted by this "in" group. The teacher could use the "think aloud" method as he/she models the use of the skill components to help the tempted student deal with the situation.

5. *Behavioral Rehearsal:*

    A. *Selection:* Two students will be selected to role play Danna and Jane from the introductory story; five or more students are required for the second role play.

    B. *Role Plays:* Role playing students will use the skill components in the following role plays.

        – Danna and Jane from the introductory story.

        – Kelly's older sister Heather has taken Kelly to hear a new-age music group they both like. Heather's two friends are there, too. It is a very special treat for Kelly to be included since she is only 11 and the other girls are 17 and 18 years old. During the concert, Kelly notices that many kids around them are smoking what looks like marijuana and passing the joints around. The boy next to Kelly taps her on the shoulder and offers her a "puff."

    C. *Completion:* After each role play, the teacher and class will decide if the appropriate behaviors were shown. If not, the role play will be re-enacted with corrections. If yes, the role play is complete.

    D. *Reinforcers:* All students will be highly praised for their role playing efforts.

    E. *Discussion:* After the role plays, the teacher will lead a discussion about marijuana. The following topics should be covered:

        ❱ **The drug marijuana is known by different names: pot, joint, grass, weed, reefer.**

        ❱ **Marijuana has harmful effects on your health and emotions.**

        ❱ **The effects of marijuana on your mind and judgment.**

        ❱ **The legal consequences of using an illegal drug such as marijuana.**

6. *Practice:* The teacher will have the students complete the worksheet "High and Dry" in class and share their responses.

7. *Independent Use:* The students will take home the worksheet "Needs and Alternatives" to discuss with their parents and record what they discussed. Responses will be shared in class.

8. *Continuation:* The teacher will stress to the children that throughout their life they will be faced with many temptations, some of which may deal with drug use. By knowing the facts about the harmful effects and the consequences of drug use, students will be better able to make an educated choice as to what is in their best interest to do.

Name _____ Date _____

HIGH AND DRY

Directions: Answer the following questions:

1. **What are some common names for marijuana?**

_____

_____

_____

_____

2. **What are the effects of marijuana on your body?**

_____

_____

_____

_____

3. **What are the effects of marijuana on your mind?**

_____

_____

_____

_____

4. **How can the consequences of marijuana use ruin your future?**

_____

_____

_____

5. **Why do some students smoke marijuana?**

_____

_____

_____

Name _____ Date _____

NEEDS AND ALTERNATIVES

Directions: Discuss with your parents the topics covered in items 1 and 2 below. Then write your responses to each item.

1. Discuss with your parents the needs, that people think they have, which cause them to take stimulants such as marijuana. Write down some of those needs here:

_____

_____

_____

_____

_____

_____

_____

_____

2. With your parents, talk about alternative activities which could fulfill the needs identified in #1. Record the alternative activities here:

_____

_____

_____

_____

_____

_____

_____

_____

_____

_____

_____
Parent

3. Ask parent(s) to sign this sheet after it is completed.

Learning About the Symptoms That Follow Stimulant Use

Behavioral Objective: Students will learn about the repulsive, uncontrollable symptoms that can be the cause of stimulant use. They will learn that even experimenting with such stimulants can have consequences for life, if addiction is the consequence as it frequently is.

Directed Lesson:

1. **Establish the Need:** Increasingly young people are exposed to people using stimulants in excess. The behavior of such persons show repulsive symptoms that are characteristic for stimulant overdoses and can be recognized. The repulsive, physical symptoms can vary from passive, belligerent, unsteady, even to violent. The mental symptoms are also displeasing. They can be spotted by noting unclear speech, too much talk and even abusive and foul language. Since the behavior of such people can become violent, children have to learn to recognize people who are under the influence of stimulant use, to avoid them or at least to avoid aggravating them. Understanding the symptoms and having learned that they cannot be controlled, children will realize that stimulant use will change their behavior in a similar manner so that they may become repulsive to their peers, family and friends. This might be an added incentive to prevent them from experimenting with stimulants.

2. **Introduction:** The teacher will read the following story:

"THE THREE MUSKETEERS"

Out of a class of 24 students, there were three boys who "hung together" on a regular basis. They were so close as friends that they came to school together, left together, and while in school ate their lunch together, sat near one another in class, and often hovered together during recess. Strangely each seemed to get into trouble at the same time. Tom was often tense and belligerent, Ray was very passive, and Ken was often very talkative, even if it meant a disruption in the class. Their teacher, Mrs. Moore, soon discovered a number of things. Tom was caught in the lavatory with a can of beer, Ken had a pocket of white stuff, and Ray whose eyes are always somewhat glassy, had been caught in class with what appeared to be a home-made cigarette that was partly burned.

The teacher will ask the class what symptoms of stimulant abuse were evident in the three students. Then, the teacher, with the assistance of the class, will identify any other symptoms and list them on the board by asking the following questions:

▶ **Do you know anyone who has been using stimulants in the neighborhood? How do you know?**

▶ **What are the symptoms or behavior of those using stimulants?**

3. *Identify the Skill Components:* Write the following skill components on the board or on sentence strips:

1. Observe the person(s) closely.

2. Evaluate the behavior and attitude.

3. Decide if the symptoms relate to stimulant or drug abuse.

4. Consider the consequences caused by such behavior.

5. Decide if this behavior can endanger you and others.

6. Understand that no person can control this behavior.

7. Realize that only abstinence returns control.

8. Understand that abstinence is most difficult after addiction.

9. Consider how others would judge you, if you show these symptoms.

10. Make a wise decision.

4. *Model the Skill:* The teacher will portray a child who looks for help, when peers use pressure and promises to make him/her participate in a smoking and drinking party. The teacher, by using the skill components, will convince him/herself to abstain from joining the party and will try to communicate the same to the peers. The teacher may select a child to be the spokesperson for the group which puts on the pressure.

5. *Behavioral Rehearsal:*

A. *Selection:* The teacher will select two pairs of children to role play.

B. *Role Plays:* The teacher will ask each pair of students to play one of the following scenarios:

- Two children will role play a conversation letting the class know what they think about the Three Musketeers from the story in the introduction and how that influenced them in their judgment regarding stimulant use.

- The other two children will be asked to make up their own role play with the help of the teacher.

C. *Completion:* After each role play, the teacher will decide if the role play was done correctly and if the skill components were used appropriately. If corrections are needed, the role play will be re-enacted; if not, the role play is complete.

D. *Reinforcers:* The teacher and class will thank the role players for their participation with applause and verbal compliments.

E. *Discussion:* The teacher will start a discussion by asking questions such as:

▶ **Did any of you experience a similar situation to that role played by the first pair of students?**

▶ **How would you react to such a group?**

▶ **Would you join and would you try to convince others to join another equally-stimulating activity?**

▶ **What would you propose?**

6. ***Practice:*** The teacher will distribute the worksheet "Repulsive" for the students to complete in class and discuss.

7. ***Independent Use:*** The teacher will distribute the worksheet "Resentment" for the students to complete at home and return in one week for discussion in class.

8. ***Continuation:*** The teacher will stress that the ugly behavior which frequently follows the use of stimulants is uncontrollable and can lead to violence and crime. Such behavior is resentful and should be avoided at all ages, no matter how great the temptation, by keeping away from indulging in the use of stimulants.

Name _____ Date _____

REPULSIVE

Directions: Please answer the following questions in full sentences:

1. What would you call the behavior that most frequently follows stimulant use? _____
   _____

2. Would you like to be a friend of anybody who shows this behavior? _____

3. Can this behavior be controlled? _____

4. Is it safe to experiment with stimulants? _____

5. Why not? _____

6. Can one try be harmful? Why? _____
   _____

7. Can you easily stop stimulant use? _____

8. What does "addiction" mean? Define it. _____
   _____

9. How does one become addicted? _____

10. Can addiction lead to violence and crime? How? _____
    _____

Write down the skill components:

1. _____

2. _____

3. _____

4. _____

5. _____

6. _____

7. _____

8. _____

9. _____

10. _____

Name _____ Date _____

RESENTMENT

Directions: For this activity, write about an actual event or make up a story along the following lines: You meet two people whose behavior indicates the after-effects of stimulant use. They scare you because they are behaving so badly that in your judgment they are at the brink of becoming abusive and violent. Tell why you think their behavior is caused by stimulant use and give reasons for your judgment and feelings. Describe why you are scared and what you will do.

Discuss your story with others (parents, friends, peers) and relate your reactions to their remarks.

Make sure to include answers to the following questions in your story:

- Would I like to befriend such a person?

- How do I prevent myself from ever behaving like this?

- Can such behavior become violent?

- When you were discussing the story with others, were there any surprises? What?

_____

_____

_____

_____

_____

_____

_____

_____

_____

_____

_____

_____

_____

_____

_____

_____

Learning to Seek Help to Stop Smoking

Behavioral Objective: The students will learn that it is illegal to buy and to smoke cigarettes if underage, and that they can be helped to stop smoking.

Directed Lesson:

1. **Establish the Need:** Too many young people think it is "cool" and "grown-up" to smoke, especially if peers smoke. Knowing that it is illegal to buy cigarettes if underage, adds a thrill to smoking because they feel they are "getting away with it." Some youngsters will even steal cigarettes or steal money and other items in order to buy cigarettes. They need to recognize the addictiveness of cigarettes and the serious health problems that can occur from smoking cigarettes. They, also, need to be aware of various types of assistance that is available to help people stop smoking.

2. **Introduction:** The teacher will read the following story to introduce this skill:

   Bonita started smoking when she was nine years old by taking puffs from the cigarettes that her friends were smoking. By her eleventh birthday, Bonita smoked a pack a day. She would smoke any time she got a chance when her parents were out of the house or while she was away from the house. She even used her lunch money to buy cigarettes along with any money she uses as gifts or that she can beg from her parents. Today, she has no money, no cigarettes and is really craving a "smoke." As she walks past the drugstore, she remembers that there is a display of cigarettes in front of and below the cash register. She wonders if she might be able to slip a pack of cigarettes into her pocket when the clerk is busy and not at the register. Bonita takes a deep breath and walks into the drugstore.

   The teacher will ask the following questions:

   ◗ **What do you think Bonita will do and what might be the consequences?**
   ◗ **What tells you that Bonita is addicted to smoking cigarettes?**
   ◗ **If you could talk to Bonita, what would you say to her about smoking?**

3. **Identify the Skill Components:** The teacher will write the skill components on the chalkboard or on a chart.

   1. Evaluate your smoking habits.
   2. Consider if you are addicted.
   3. Think about the consequences of continuing to smoke.
   4. Decide if you want help to stop smoking.

5. Examine what help is available to stop smoking.

6. Seek the help you need to stop smoking.

4. ***Model the Skill:*** The teacher will model Bonita from the introductory story as he/she uses the skill components to make a decision about smoking. By using the "think aloud" method, the teacher can demonstrate how the skill components can be applied to the thought process of making a decision.

5. ***Behavioral Rehearsal:***

   A. *Selection:* The teacher will select two students for each of two role plays.

   B. *Role Plays:* The teacher will give each pair of students one of the following scenarios.

      – James, who does not smoke, uses the skill components to help his friend Kevin, who does smoke, make a decision about whether to continue smoking or to quit smoking.

      – Carla is concerned because her father smokes a lot. Expressing her concern for his health, Carla uses the skill components to discuss smoking with her father.

   C. *Completion:* The teacher and the class will determine if the role play was done correctly and if the appropriate skills were used. If not, the teacher will ask the students to re-enact the role play with corrections. If yes, the role play is complete.

   D. *Reinforcers:* The teacher will use praise or other age-appropriate rewards to acknowledge the students' participation and attitude.

   E. *Discussion:* After the two role plays, the teacher will ask the students the following questions:

      ❯ **Why do you think James and Carla are involving themselves in another person's habit of smoking?**

      ❯ **What problems could James and Carla face in discussing smoking with Kevin and Father?**

      ❯ **What do you think you would do if a friend wanted you to start smoking?**

6. ***Practice:*** Distribute copies of the worksheet "Up in Smoke" for students to complete and discuss in class.

7. ***Independent Use:*** As an out-of-class assignment, the teacher will ask the students to develop a poster with wording that portrays a fact or facts about cigarette smoking. The poster should be at least 12″ × 18″ in size. Posters with a message can be displayed in the classroom or in the school's halls. The class will vote on the best poster, which will get a prize.

8. ***Continuation:*** The teacher will emphasize that it is in one's best interest not to smoke or to stop smoking if already doing so. Encourage children to consider the cost of smoking to one's health as well as monetary costs. The teacher will remind children that the smoking habit or addiction can be treated by a variety of methods available for both youngsters and adults. He/she will stress that their present and future activities depend heavily on being in good health.

Name _____ Date _____

UP IN SMOKE

Directions: Unscramble these words that about smoking cigarettes. (Turn this page upside down for help.)

1. **Eplh** _____

2. **kmeos** _____

3. **arecgittse** _____

4. **hbiat** _____

5. **ilgella** _____

6. **htheal** _____

7. **adddtice** _____

8. **pots** _____

9. **icks** _____

10. **ffup** _____

Answers: addicted, cigarettes, habit, health, help, illegal, puff, sick, smoke, stop

Understanding the Consequences Due to Inhaling

Behavioral Objective: Students will learn that they can become deadly sick when they use everyday household items as inhalants and that some people have paid with their lives for such misuse.

Directed Lesson:

1. ***Establish the Need:*** Students like to feel "high" and "giggly" especially if prompted to do so by a group of their peers. They know that inhaling the odor of some ordinary household items, which are easy to get and are cheap, will produce this sensation. Children have to learn to understand that inhaling any of those items is extremely dangerous to their health and can cause imminent death. The younger the children, the less they will understand the danger they are exposed to when inhaling since they think, "at my age nothing serious can ever happen to me." Neither do they realize how difficult it will be to avoid using inhalants after the first try. Therefore, it is very necessary that they understand the serious consequences due to inhaling such items as for example, correction white-out and lighter fluid, which are lying around in many homes and are available in almost any office. It is of vital importance that children know the serious consequence of a first try at using inhalants and act accordingly.

2. ***Introduction:*** The teacher will read the following story:

   Tommy just got a new video game for his play-station. He invited his best friends, Joey and Michael, to come to his house and play the game with him. While they were playing the game, Joey told Michael and Tommy that you could get "high" by inhaling the smell that comes from a jar of rubber cement.

   All three boys decided to try inhaling the rubber cement. As they did, they felt kind of giggly and everything they said or did seemed funny. They all liked the fun they were having and decided to find other household products to inhale to see if it felt the same way.

   For the next few days, Tommy would meet with the same group of friends. Each day they had something different that they used to inhale to get high. One day, it was smelling fumes from a metallic paint can, other days it was air freshener, the glue and even white-out correction fluid.

   After inhaling for a few days, each day spending more time together and inhaling many different household items at the same time, Tommy got very sick, vomiting first and fainting later. The other boys had to get him home. He did not recover and had to be taken to a hospital. In the hospital it took the doctors two days to stabilize him. Finally he realized the seriousness of his condition and pledged to himself never to repeat this experience.

The teacher will ask the following questions:

-) **What could have happened to Tommy?**
-) **How bad was Tommy's experience?**
-) **Will it be easy for Tommy to keep his promise?**
-) **Did you learn from Tommy's experience?**

3. ***Identify the Skill Components:*** Write the following skill components on the board or on sentence strips.

1. Consider the reasons for joining a questionable group activity.

2. Analyze the consequences of participating in the activity.

3. Weigh the pleasure against the harm.

4. Consider longtime consequences upon your future.

5. Think of a substitute activity.

6. Make a careful decision.

4. ***Model the Skill:*** The teacher will ask one student from the class to portray the role of someone who is tempted by some of his classmates to inhale some easily available products in order to join the "fun" of a group. The teacher will use the skill components to guide the student in making his/her own decision.

5. ***Behavioral Rehearsal:***

A. *Selection:* The teacher will select two sets of three students for enacting role plays.

B. *Role Plays:* The teacher will ask each set of the students to role play one of the following scenarios, using the skill components.

- – Role playing the story in the lesson's introduction of Tommy, Michael and Joey inhaling various household products.

- – While playing in their father's garage, Mary and her two friends find several items that they know can be used to have a "funny feeling" after they inhale their smell. They are wondering and discussing how it would feel, and are tempted to try inhaling the smell of these items.

C. *Completion:* After each role play, the teacher will reinforce correct behaviors, identify inappropriate behaviors and ask the students to re-enact the role play with corrections, if necessary. If there are no corrections, the role play is complete.

D. *Reinforcers:* The teacher will give verbal and non-verbal praise (specific) for correct role plays.

E. *Discussion:* The teacher will lead the discussion by asking the following questions:

-) **What can be the consequences for using household products for inhaling?**
-) **Why do you think that people like to try to get high?**
-) **How sick can you get from inhaling the smell of household products?**
-) **Do you think that the pleasure is worth the sick feeling?**
-) **Could you think of an activity that you could do in a group which would give you equal or even more pleasure?**

6. ***Practice:*** The teacher will distribute either of the two worksheets "Temptation" or "Search It Out" and ask students to complete and discuss it in class.

7. ***Independent Use:*** The teacher will distribute either of the two worksheets "Most Commonly Used Products" or "Home Project—Parent Child Project" to complete at home and bring back in one week for discussion in class.

8. ***Continuation:*** The teacher will keep reminding the students that these common household goods are especially dangerous since they contain impurities that can affect muscles, nerves and brain cells and thus cause physical, nervous and mental symptoms that are irreversible and can last the entire life or lead to death.

Name _____ Date _____

TEMPTATION

Directions: Write down the six skill components. Answer the following five questions in complete sentences.

1. _____
2. _____
3. _____
4. _____
5. _____
6. _____

1. If a group of your friends asks you to join in an inhaling party, what would you think of doing?

_____

_____

2. How would you manage to resist the peer pressure?

_____

_____

3. Could you think of joining another group of friends? Why Yes? Why No?

_____

_____

4. Can you think of a group activity you would especially enjoy? Name the activity(ies).

_____

_____

5. Would the above activity keep you from the temptation? Why?

_____

_____

_____

Name _____   Date _____

SEARCH IT OUT

Directions: Often, there are household items of danger to ourselves in our own homes. Visit each of the 4 rooms of this house in your mind, list a dangerous product that might be found in each of the rooms listed. Write down a different product for each room. Students will then discuss what they found and . . . be able to tell how to safely store it or how to avoid its abuse.

① BEDROOM: _____

② BATHROOM: _____

③ KITCHEN: _____

④ BASEMENT: _____

Name _____ Date _____

MOST COMMONLY USED PRODUCTS

Directions:

1. Draw pictures of six commonly used household products in the six boxes below. Write next to each picture what purpose the item serves and where it is usually found in the home. Under "Remarks," place an asterisk (*) if you think the product can serve as an inhalant and use the numbers from 0 to 5 to indicate how sick you can become if you use it as an inhalant (0 indicates not sick at all and 5 indicates extremely ill).

PICTURE	PURPOSE	LOCATION	REMARKS

Name _____ Date _____

MOST COMMONLY USED PRODUCTS *(Continued)*

2. Tell if you would be tempted to inhale if friends pressured you to do it as a group activity or if you never can be tempted to join an inhalant party.

   _____

   _____

3. Tell how you know what can be used as an inhalant and how to use it.

   _____

   _____

4. Tell about other group activities that make you feel equal or even more "high" than inhaling and why they do so.

   _____

   _____

5. Discuss this worksheet with your parent(s) and describe how they reacted to your comments.

   _____

   _____

   _____

   _____

   _____

   _____

   _____

   _____

   _____

   _____

   _____

Name _____ Date _____

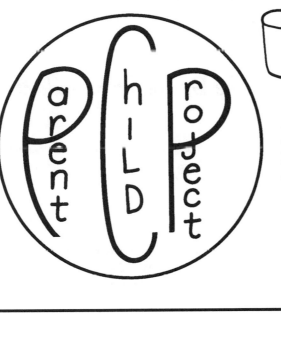

Directions: We have discussed how some common household products found in the home can be addictive or misused to produce danger.

- The parent or guardian will help identify such a product with their son/daughter. Then, cut out and affix the label in the space provided, tell briefly how it can hurt us and how one can avoid its misuse.

What can happen if it is misused?

_____

_____

_____

_____

_____

_____

Paste Product Label here
or
**draw the label if it cannot be
removed**

How can we avoid its misuse?

_____

_____

_____

_____

_____

_____

_____

_____

Selecting Activities to Conquer the Desire for Stimulant Use

Behavioral Objective: Students will learn to engage in mentally exciting and wholesome activities to counteract the desire for using stimulants which are most likely to produce negative effects and can destroy all pleasure in life.

Directed Lesson:

1. **Establish the Need:** Today, nearly 1.5 million children and adolescents are depressed to the point that they rely on drugs to counteract their feelings. And, this figure represents only those who are relying on prescription drugs. Others depend on various over-the-counter medications, stimulants and drugs. Many do become "hooked" on illegal drugs and other stimulants; many of the latter are common household products. As a result, violence becomes a natural outgrowth of such a dependency. Children will learn that there are activities available in which they can participate that are equally exciting or more so and much healthier, and with less dangerous consequences than any use of stimulants.

2. **Introduction:** The teacher will ask the students to assist in completing a chart such as that on page 151. The teacher will ask a student to copy the chart on the board or use an overhead projector to project it on the wall.

   The teacher will explain about the immediate and long-time consequences by giving the children an example and will also tell them what is meant by expected excitement and danger. The purpose of the chart when completed, is to show the children that there are many exciting activities to choose from, rather than participating in a drug party, which are more fun and have no dangerous consequences.

   The teacher will then ask the following questions:

   ▶ **What activities would you prefer? Let us first list them on the board and then assign priority numbers.**

   ▶ **Which of the activities do you think will be most exciting? Let us again assign priorities but this time with letters.**

   ▶ **Which are the activities you agree on to be most preferred and believe to be most exciting?**

3. **Identify the Skill Components:** Write the following skill components on the board or on sentence strips:

   1. Consider the reason(s) or need to take stimulants.

   2. Analyze what consideration led to the desire.

   3. Understand the immediate consequences.

4. Consider the long-term consequences.

5. Investigate other activities that could produce the same excitement.

6. Consider the consequences inherent in those activities.

7. Weigh the excitement and consequences.

8. Choose wisely.

4. ***Model the Skill:*** The teacher will select one student to portray the leader of a group of classmates, who tries to convince him/her, role playing another classmate, to join in a "stimulant" party of "special fun." The teacher will try to convince him/herself by using the skill components to select a healthy activity instead and will show how and why such a decision was made.

5. ***Behavioral Rehearsal:***

   A. *Selection:* The teacher will select two pairs of students to role play.

   B. *Role Plays:* The role plays will have the following scenarios:

       – Ted encouraging Albert, a heavy-set sad boy, to smoke some "weed."

       – Mary, a fourth grader, and her mother live in a basement apartment. The mother is divorced and is an alcoholic and tells Mary to take occasional sips.

   C. *Completion:* After each role play, the teacher will decide if the role play was done correctly and if the skill components were used appropriately. If corrections are needed, the role play will be re-enacted; if not, the role play is complete.

   D. *Reinforcers:* The teacher and class will thank the role players for their participation with applause and verbal praise.

   E. *Discussion:* The teacher will again review consequences of different activities. The teacher will then ask questions such as:

     ▶ **If somebody tempts you to take stimulants, what will you do?**

     ▶ **Are some activities more exciting than others? Why?**

     ▶ **What are the consequences that can occur when partaking in healthy activities?**

     ▶ **What consequences may occur after participating in forbidden activities?**

     ▶ **Do you find the skill components useful?**

6. ***Practice:*** The teacher will distribute the worksheet "Alternatives—Staying Away from Stimulants" and instruct the students to complete the assignment and share their responses in class.

7. ***Independent Use:*** The teacher will distribute the worksheet "Drugs or What? For students to do at home and to discuss with their parent(s). The student will be asked to return the poster in one week and share with the class. The posters may be hung in the hall for the entire school population to admire and learn from their messages.

8. ***Continuation:*** The teacher will emphasize that in life, frequent temptations are great for activities that are unlawful and should be avoided. In such cases, the best way is to weigh the consequences and then find an equally satisfactory, clean activity to substitute for the temptation, as is being done in this lesson. Therefore, this skill will serve all people well during their entire lives.

ACTIVITIES COMPARISON CHART

	FUN	EXPECTED EXCITEMENT	CONSEQUENCES		DANGER	LEGAL
			IMMEDIATE	LONG-TERM		
Playing a Computer Game						
Skiing						
Hiking						
Drinking Beer						
Playing Catch						
Painting						
Smoking Marijuana						
Bicycle Racing						
Playing a Game of Cards						
Inhaling Rubber Cement						
Swimming						
Playing Baseball						
Roller-Skating						
Choral Singing						
Doing a Crossword Puzzle						
Others						

Name _____ Date _____

ALTERNATIVES—STAYING AWAY FROM STIMULANTS

Directions: Draw pictures of four (4) activities you can do instead of trying stimulants.

Music	**Sport**
Hobby/Crafts	**Game(s)**

Name _____ Date _____

DRUGS OR WHAT?

Directions: Create a poster with two drawings on a separate sheet of heavy paper or cardboard. One drawing can be a cartoon or other animated character, such as Pluto or Donald Duck, with a message warning of the danger of stimulant abuse.

Sample

The second drawing should portray a healthy activity such as bicycling or team sports, with a message indicating how much fun one can have doing it and how invigorated it makes you feel.

Sample

Write a message about what you learned from the skill in this lesson and from comparing the messages in the two drawings, such as: The Poster shows . . .

Discuss the poster with your parent(s).

_____

_____

_____

_____

Learning to Seek Help Against Addiction

Behavioral Objective: Students will learn that trusted adults are willing to assist them to break away from taking stimulants but only if they themselves have the wish to discontinue the dangerous and unhealthy habit and therefore ask for such assistance.

Directed Lesson:

1. **Establish the Need:** Youngsters are frequently tempted to experiment with all kinds of stimulants. Sometimes, they are enticed by curiosity but most often they are provoked by peers or adults who already are addicted. Children have to understand that it is important to avoid even "a first time" experimentation since some people get addicted instantly and believe that they cannot live without stimulants after the first try. Usually they get deeper and deeper into the habit of using stimulants without realizing what happened to them. Stimulants cost money and that might lead to shoplifting, stealing and other criminal acts. Therefore, students have to learn not only to recognize their addiction but to know that help is available if they are willing to discontinue the dangerous habit and ask to be helped. It is important for children to understand that it is never shameful to ask for assistance.

2. **Introduction:** The teacher will read the following story to the class:

   Clifford and Gary had been in the same classes from Kindergarten right up to the fifth grade. They knew each other very well and were good friends. As they began their fifth grade school year, Clifford noticed that Gary began changing. His behavior was not the same and he didn't care about anything.

   Over the summer vacation, Gary began smoking cigarettes and drinking beer and wine coolers. He told Clifford that it made him feel good when he smoked cigarettes and drank. Gary said it's "cool" to get "high" and that he should try it with him.

   Clifford watched how Gary, who used to be a good student, was now always getting into trouble at school. He was now failing all of his classes, and started stealing and extorting money from his classmates so that he could have some to buy his beer and cigarettes.

   One day after he had been drinking and was out of control, Gary got on his bike and rode it down a street that had a lot of traffic. Cars had to swerve, and drivers had to hit their brakes as Gary acted like nothing could hurt him. He turned his bike to avoid the truck, then found himself turning over and landing on the concrete street.

   Clifford had seen what happened and rushed to help Gary as he lay bleeding and crying on the street. Clifford told him that he had to break away from smoking and drinking because if he didn't, it was going to kill him. Gary realized that Clifford meant well for him. However, Gary did not know that he was addicted and how he could stop his bad habits, but he started to think about what he should do.

153

The teacher will ask the following questions:

> **Was Gary addicted?**

> **How do you think Gary was able to break away from his drug addiction?**

3. *Identify the Skill Components:* Write the following skill components on the board, on transparencies to be used with an overhead projector, or on sentence strips:

1. Evaluate the situation.

2. Identify the reasons for using stimulants.

3. Analyze the pleasures.

4. Analyze the harm to you and to others.

5. Consider the consequences.

6. Decide if you are addicted.

7. Decide if you need help.

8. Ask a trusted adult to help.

9. Follow through.

4. *Model the Skill:* The teacher will portray Gary from the story in the lesson's introduction and will ask a child to role play Clifford. With the use of the skill components, Gary will decide that asking for help is the best step to take to shed the addiction.

5. *Behavioral Rehearsal:*

A. *Selection:* The teacher will select two groups of an appropriate number of children to perform the following two role plays.

B. *Role Plays:* Each group of students will role play one of the following scenarios:

- A group of children meet secretly every day after school to drink, smoke or inhale for a good time together. One afternoon one of the children feels very sick and faints. The others have to call the police. Thus the whole town will soon know about their secret habits. What to do?

- A shopowner catches two children shoplifting and tells the children that he will take them to the police if he ever finds them doing the same again. The children need money to buy cigarettes. They feel they cannot live without smoking. What will they do next?

C. *Completion:* After each role play, the teacher will decide if the role play was done correctly and if the skill components were used appropriately. If corrections are needed, the role plays will be re-enacted; if not, the role play is complete.

D. *Reinforcers:* The teacher and class will thank the role players for their participation with applause and verbal praise.

E. *Discussion:* The teacher will begin a discussion by asking the following questions:

> **Is it shameful to ask for help?**

> **Would it not have been much better to avoid stimulant use altogether?**

> **Do you realize how difficult it is to break such a habit?**

> **Have any of you an idea how this is done?**

These questions should lead to a discussion of addiction versus avoidance and to the conclusion that if they are addicted they need help to break the habit and should not be ashamed to ask for it.

6. *Practice:* The teacher will distribute the worksheet "Please Help" for the students to complete and to discuss their answers in class.

7. *Independent Use:* The teacher will distribute the worksheet "Double Trouble" for the students to complete at home and ask them to return it completed in one week for discussing it in class

8. *Continuation:* The teacher will emphasize that it is best to avoid stimulant use. However, if they have experimented with stimulants and become addicted, they should not be ashamed and reluctant to ask for help from an adult since to break away from an addiction is very difficult and almost impossible to do unless helped by treatment. The teacher will also indicate that addiction at any age will require professional help.

Name _____ Date _____

PLEASE HELP

Directions: Answer the following questions:

1. If you want to break an addiction, what will

   you do? _____

2. Whom would you ask? (List several people)

   _____

   _____

3. How would you ask? _____

4. Is it necessary to get help? Why? _____

5. How will you avoid addiction? _____

6. How difficult is it to break addiction? _____

7. If peers ask you to join in stimulant use, what would your answer be?

   _____

8. Do you think you can handle peer pressure? _____

9. How will you handle peer pressure? _____

Write down the skill components:

1. _____

2. _____

3. _____

4. _____

5. _____

6. _____

7. _____

8. _____

9. _____

Name _____ Date _____

DOUBLE TROUBLE

Directions:

1. Describe a situation where one or more children have done something wrong because of addiction and are in the process of getting into trouble and tell why they decide to break with the bad habit and how they will accomplish this. Discuss this story with your parent(s).

_____

_____

_____

_____

_____

_____

_____

_____

_____

_____

_____

_____

_____

2. Answer the following questions:

– Did you use the skill components to write your story? _____

– Did they assist you? _____

– What did your parent(s) say? _____

_____

_____

_____

Learning to Change Bully Behavior

Behavioral Objective: Bullies, when ignored by all the other kids, will want to change their behavior in order to make friends. Bullies will learn that in order to change their behavior, they have to acquire self-esteem and social grace.

Directed Lesson:

1. **Establish the Need:** In almost every class there is a bully; often more than one. The other children become the bully's sidekick, victim, and bystander. Children can learn to ignore bullies by paying no attention to them. If they do so, the bullies will want to change their behavior in order to make friends with the other kids. Bullies usually want control and power and know no other way to assert themselves but to use threats and ridicule to get what they want. Bullies have to learn that children who have self-esteem and social grace can get all they want without violence and threats. They also have to realize that children who do not stop their bully behavior at a young age may have the tendency to become delinquent and violent as adolescents and adults. Therefore, it is important for bullies to change their behavior and to learn how to deal peacefully with their peers.

2. **Introduction:** The teacher will read the following story to the class:

   Chuck was in the third grade. He had two older brothers and one younger sister. His older brothers were always picking on him, calling him names, hitting him, breaking his toys and taking his money. His parents would not listen to him when he complained about what his brothers did to him. One day on the way to school, Chuck's brothers tore up his homework and took his lunch money. Chuck was not only mad, but he was humiliated because some other boys from school saw what happened. Chuck clenched his fists and ordered himself not to cry, but he was fuming. Then he saw Philip, a quiet boy from his class. He went up to Philip, demanded his homework paper and lunch money. Philip started to protest, but Chuck shoved his fist into Philip's face and said that Philip better give him the paper and money or else! Philip gave him what he wanted. Chuck warned Philip not to tell or Chuck would "get" him. He smiled to himself as he continued on to school. As Chuck walked away, he felt satisfied, powerful, in control. Three other children saw what happened but said nothing then or at school.

   The teacher will use the following questions to lead a discussion about Chuck and bullies:

   ▶ **How was Chuck treated by his older brothers? Parents?**
   ▶ **Why did Chuck treat Philip as he did?**
   ▶ **Was Chuck becoming a bully himself? Why?**
   ▶ **Why do you think Chuck was smiling after he left Philip?**

> **What was happening to Chuck?**
> **What should Philip do?**
> **Is there anything the bystanders could have done?**

Some ideas the teacher can mention during the discussion could be:

- Bullies sometimes do not feel good about themselves. (low self-esteem)
- Bullies pick on others to make them think they are better.
- Bullies feel good when they are in control.
- Bullies think the only way to get what you want is to take it.

3. ***Identify the Skill Components:*** Write the following skill components on the board, chart or sentence strips:

1. Decide if you are a bully.

2. Think why you are bullying others.

3. Consider how bullying hurts all involved.

4. Consider that others might like you if you would stop being a bully.

5. Think about what you can do to change yourself.

6. Think about how you can be assertive without being a bully.

7. Get help from a caring parent or other trusted adult.

4. ***Model the Skill:*** The teacher will draw from his/her elementary school days to recall an incident involving a bully. After relating the incident to the class, the teacher will follow the skill components and show how the bully realized that he/she had to change to find a friend.

5. ***Behavioral Rehearsal:***

   A. *Selection:* The teacher will select the appropriate number of students needed for the role plays.

   B. *Role Plays:*

   - Students can role play Chuck, Chuck's brothers and Philip from the introductory story. They can show how to use the skill components to have a different ending of the story.

   - For a whole week, Susan has been bullied by Amy. Amy trips her, pulls her hair and pours juice or milk on Susan's lunch. Susan just doesn't understand; they used to be friends.

   - On the playground, Joseph, Devon, Jamal and Steve, all fifth graders, saw Harry, a sixth grader, bullying a first grade boy. They walked over to where this was happening.

   C. *Completion:* Following each role play, the teacher will reinforce correct behaviors, identify inappropriate behaviors and have the children re-enact the role play with corrections, if needed. If there are no corrections, the role play is complete.

    D. *Reinforcers:* The teacher and class will give applause and high praise to the role players.

    E. *Discussion:* The teacher will discuss with the children how to ignore a bully and emphasize that bullies have to learn to feel good about themselves to achieve some degree of control without resorting to aggression or violence. The teacher may also give the children some names of persons who could help to avoid an incident of bullying.

6. *Practice:* The teacher will distribute the worksheet "Dejected Bully" and ask the children to draw pictures and to complete the directions in class. On completion, the teacher will ask the students to tell their thoughts to the class.

7. *Independent Use:* The teacher will distribute the worksheet "Help For Change" to the children to take home and return completed in one week for discussion in class.

8. *Continuation:* The teacher will continue to reinforce the skill components as needed and remind students that children who are bullies can grow up to be adult bullies and get into trouble with the law because of their actions. The teacher will help them to understand that it is easier and more beneficial to change behaviors while young.

Name _____ Date _____

DEJECTED BULLY

Directions: Draw pictures of a bully and children at play in the two boxes below. Then describe the feelings, in full sentences, of the children playing together and those of the lonely bully. Don't you think the bully would like to join the other children?

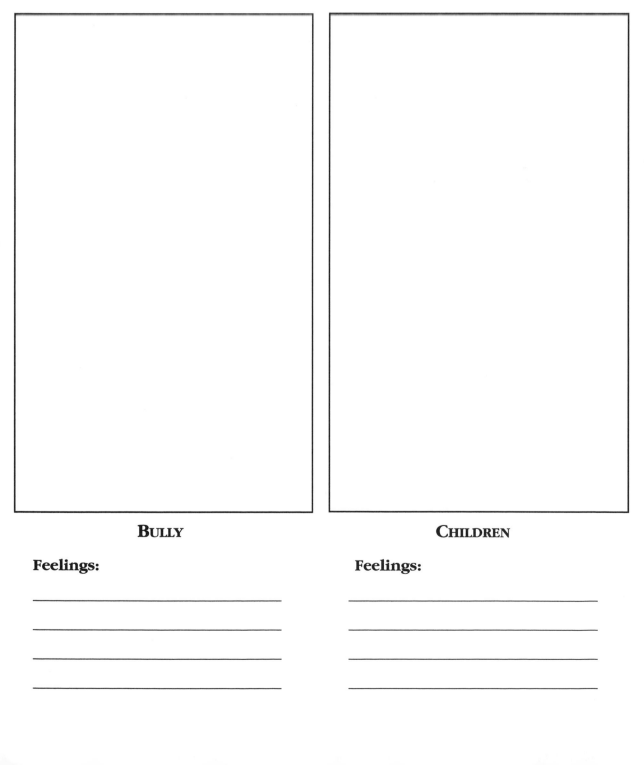

BULLY

CHILDREN

Feelings:

Feelings:

_____

_____

_____

_____

_____

_____

_____

_____

Name _____ Date _____

NEED HELP FOR CHANGE?

Directions: Write down the eight skill components and what you think about each. If you think you are a bully, write how you feel; if you think you are not a bully, write about how you feel about the bully. Tell if the skill components could help to change the bully's behavior. Talk about your thoughts with your parents. (If necessary, use the back of this page.) Have the parent(s) sign this sheet and on the back.

Skill Components

1. _____
2. _____
3. _____
4. _____
5. _____
6. _____
7. _____
8. _____

Your thoughts:

_____

_____

_____

_____

_____

Parent(s) suggestions:

_____

_____

_____

_____

_____

_____
Parent

Understanding the Difference Between Need and Desire

Behavioral Objective: Students will learn to understand what the essential needs are that make them function as members of society and that, only after those needs are met, desires and wants can be satisfied if they are obtainable without adverse consequences.

Directed Lesson:

1. **Establish the Need:** Many children, and also adults, have no clear understanding about their basic needs for survival and their excessive desires to shine and/or to fit in with the crowd. They can never get enough. After their basic needs are met, they strive for all kinds of material goodies, such as computer games, bicycles, ornaments, fancy clothes and so on. Sometimes the desire becomes so great that they will participate in violent and illegal activities, such as fights, theft, robbery, and even assault to obtain the wanted objects. Children must learn that they can only have the items their family can afford and is willing to give them and that partaking in illegal activities to obtain objects of desire can lead to painful consequences that could ruin their entire future lives.

2. **Introduction:** The teacher will read the following story:

   Michael, age 10, and his three sisters, ages 8, 9 and 12, live with their mother in a small two-bedroom apartment. The mother works and comes home late every evening. The four children have to help clean the apartment and have to learn to take care of their own needs. Michael, being the only boy, cannot inherit clothes from the sister. Therefore his mother buys all his clothes in a second-hand store. Michael's schoolmates notice that his tennis shoes are worn and old-fashioned and brag about their own new fashionable shoes. This irritates Michael. Julius, the biggest bragger of all, also a boy from a family of small means, suggests that Michael can have new tennis shoes if he accompanies him to stake out stores. He claims that they can easily shoplift sufficient small items to afford new tennis shoes for both of them. Michael is tempted.

   The teacher might ask:

   ◗ **Are new tennis shoes an essential need?**

   ◗ **Why is Michael's desire aroused?**

   ◗ **What do you think Michael will do?**

3. **Identify the Skill Components:** Write the following skill components on the board or on sentence strips:

   1. Define essential needs.

   2. Consider your desires and wants.

3. Think about how those desires were created.

4. Consider how to satisfy your desires.

5. Think about the consequences.

6. Study the pros and cons.

7. Make an appropriate decision.

4. ***Model the Skill:*** The teacher will talk about a time when he/she was close to the age of his/her class and had a great desire to own a certain item that his/her family could not afford to purchase. By using the skill components the teacher will go through a thought process to show the children how to make a proper decision.

The teacher will follow up this lesson by asking the children to brainstorm needs and wants and have one child write the needs on the left side of the chalkboard and the wants or desires on the right-hand side. The teacher might also discuss how important it is to decide between essential objects and those desired and that life can be pleasant without the ful-fillment of all desires.

5. ***Behavioral Rehearsal:***

A. *Selection:* The teacher will select three groups of six children.

B. *Role Plays:* Each group of six children will role play Michael, the three sisters, the mother and Julius. By using the skill components, each group of role players will be asked to complete the story with variations.

C. *Completion:* After each role play, reinforce correct behavior, identify inappropriate behaviors and re-enact role play with corrections. If there are no corrections, the role play is complete.

D. *Reinforcers:* Give verbal and nonverbal praise (specific) for correct behavior.

E. *Discussion:* The teacher will lead the discussion by asking:

> **What are the consequences for illegal activities?**
> **Is it worthwhile to satisfy the desire by participating in such activities?**
> **Are there other ways to satisfy dreams of desire?**
> **Is happiness possible without getting all you want?**
> **How will you face classmates who tempt you to do things to fulfill your desires that you know are wrong?**

6. ***Practice:*** The teacher will distribute the worksheet "Desire" and ask the students to complete it in class and discuss.

7. ***Independent Use:*** The teacher will hand out the worksheet "A Wish" to take home and ask the children to return it in one week for discussion in class.

8. ***Continuation:*** The teacher will tell the children that unfulfilled wishes will be problems during their entire lives and that they will have to learn to cope with unfulfilled desires and make the best of it to enjoy life. The teacher will emphasize always to think of conse-quences when being tempted to fulfill desires for non-essentials.

Name _____ Date _____

DESIRE

Directions: Tell about an actual or invented occurrence when you were tempted to get something you very much desired which your family could not afford.

What did you desire?

_____

_____

Who was involved besides yourself?

_____

_____

Did you decide to fulfill your desire? _____

    If yes, what did you do?

    _____

    If no, why not?

    _____

What would you do now?

_____

Did you use the skill components to make a decision? How?

_____

_____

_____

_____

_____

_____

_____

Name _____ Date _____

A WISH

Directions: Dream of an unfulfilled wish you had over a long time and describe it. Then use the skill components to help you to make a decision on how to handle the desire. Tell in complete paragraphs the decision you made and its consequences. Discuss the decision with your parents and tell about this discussion.

Your wish _____

_____

_____

Decision _____

_____

Consequences _____

_____

Write in the skill components you used.

1. _____

2. _____

3. _____

4. _____

5. _____

6. _____

7. _____

Discussion with parents: _____

_____

Learning to Be Selective with Media Programs

Behavioral Objective: Children will learn to be selective when listening to media programs, especially on the television and the Internet. They will become aware that some programs are full of trash, sex, violence and dangers, such as dating strangers, and thus are not worth being selected and should be cut when they accidentally come on the screen.

Directed Lesson:

1. **Establish the Need:** Children frequently do not realize the amount of "trash" and danger communicated by media programs. In addition, they sometimes are greatly attracted to trash, especially when it is portrayed by abundant sex, violence and danger. On the internet, there is an added danger of interacting with strangers and conversing about most intimate matters. Children have to learn to become astute and to avoid such programs since learning from them can misguide them and provoke serious behavioral problems of abuse and violence leading possibly to impaired health and violent encounters.

2. **Introduction:** The teacher will read the following story:

   Aaron, age 9, and Sam, age 8, were watching television one Friday evening. Their parents thought they were old enough to leave them for a few hours. They were never left alone more than that, but they were responsible boys. They liked the sitcoms mostly and, of course, cartoons. While using the remote they came across a movie that caught their attention immediately. Wow, this showed more than the kissing that they had seen in other movies. Then, all of a sudden, two men shot through the window and blasted the entire room and killed the couple. Aaron was staring at the television and Sam said that he did not want to watch such trash. Aaron wanted to continue watching the movie, saying this kind of "stuff" is on the news all of the time. Sam does not want Aaron to think he is a sissy, but why watch such a movie?

   The teacher will then ask:

   ▶ **What do you think about such programs?**
   ▶ **Who would listen to it? Why?**
   ▶ **What should Sam have done?**

3. **Identify the Skill Components:** Write the following skill components on the board or on sentence strips.

   1. Be selective when using the media.
   2. Consider the time you have.
   3. Analyze what the program communicates to you.
   4. Think about its actual contents.

5. Examine the possible consequences.

6. Decide if you gain or lose spending time with it.

7. Decide if there is a better way to spend time.

4. **Model the Skill:** The teacher will role play Aaron and ask a student to play Sam. The teacher role playing Aaron will use the skill components to make his/her decision, which might please Sam. Sam can also help by prodding Aaron.

5. **Behavioral Rehearsal:**

A. *Selection:* The teacher will select three pairs of students to role play.

B. *Role Plays:* Each pair will role play one of the following scenarios:

— Two students surf the Internet and discover a lonely hearts club. This perks their interest and the students have to decide what to do next.

— Two students sit in front of the television wondering which program they want to watch. One clicks the automatic selector switch "on" and "off" until he/she finds an extremely violent show with multiple shootings and killings. He/she likes this program and keeps the television on this channel. The other student feels that this program is trash and wants to look at something else.

— Two students find, on the Internet, a recipe for making explosives and setting them off. One is excited about the topic, the other wants to keep browsing, knowing that the parents would not cherish his/her interest in such a program.

C. *Completion:* After each role play, the teacher will reinforce correct behavior, identify inappropriate behavior and ask the students to re-enact the role play if corrections are needed. If there are no corrections, the role play is complete.

D. *Reinforcers:* The teacher will thank the students for their performance, and the class will compliment the role players. Applause is appropriate and necessary.

E. *Discussion:* The teacher will lead the discussion with the following questions:

▶ **Why are there so many violent programs on television?**

▶ **Why do you think it is dangerous to watch programs with a violent or indecent content?**

▶ **Why are many of you so interested in programs that are indecent and/or violent?**

▶ **If you come across any of those subjects when browsing the Internet, what will you do?**

6. **Practice:** The teacher will distribute the worksheet "Program Preference" to be done in class and to be discussed in class after completion.

7. **Independent Use:** The teacher will distribute the worksheet "Daily Calendar" and ask the students to complete it at home and to discuss it with their parent(s). Students will be asked to return it in one week for discussion in class.

8. **Continuation:** The teacher will remind the students of the importance of making appropriate choices when selecting programs, not only to maximize the time they have for extracurricular learning, but mainly to avoid wasting time on trash and to avoid being influenced and tempted in participating in activities that are indecent, illegal and dangerous.

Name _____ Date _____

PROGRAM PREFERENCE

Directions: Write one paragraph each about two television programs which you especially like. Tell why you like each program and what you can learn by viewing it. Separately, tell what information and programs you browse for on the Internet and why you select them. Finally, answer the question below.

Television Program #1 _____

_____

_____

Television Program #2 _____

_____

_____

Internet Information _____

_____

_____

Internet Programs _____

_____

Question: Will your preference for programs change after this lesson? Why yes? Why no?

_____

_____

_____

_____

_____

_____

_____

_____

_____

_____

Name _____ Date _____

DAILY CALENDAR

Directions: Write down for three days of one week the best and worst programs you watched on television and the best and worst information or programs you came upon when browsing the Internet. Also, indicate why you rated it "best" or "worst," what you learned from it, how much time you spent with it, and which skill components helped you to do the rating. Discuss your program choices with your parent(s). Have a parent sign this sheet.

	Day You Watched or Browsed	Subject	Why Did You Give It This Rating?	What Did You Learn?	Time Spent	Skill Component Used
TV Best						
TV Worst						
Internet Best						
Internet Worst						

Parent comments: _____

_____

_____

_____

_____

_____

Parent

Satisfying a Need for Thrills by Joining Lawful Activities

Behavioral Objective: Students will learn that when they look for great excitement in play and fun, that there is a large choice of many socially-accepted (non-criminal) activities creating high thrills and daring adventures, which they can join to satisfy their needs.

Directed Lesson:

1. **Establish the Need:** Young people sometimes participate in behaviors that result in petty crimes because they desire daring and exciting activities. They may take other people's belongings, harass others for the "fun of it," play harmful pranks, etc. Youngsters need to learn that such behaviors can actually be illegal, violent and may cause harm to themselves and others. These behaviors could lead to involvement with the juvenile court system and serious punishment, such as detention. Therefore youngsters should learn about the many non-criminal activities that are available and can satisfy their craving for excitement and high thrills.

2. **Introduction:** The teacher will read the following story to the class:

   Devon and Tyrone were discussing how the people on TV and in the movies rob stores and hold up people and never get caught. They thought that it didn't look too hard to do and thought that getting away with doing such things could be exciting and fun. Devon and Tyrone played that they were robbing the local drugstore.

   One day while at the drugstore, Devon and Tyrone decided to steal some candy just to see if they could get away with it. They walked around the store looking at things and slipped the candy into their pockets; then they bought a pack of gum. Once outside, they laughed about how easy it was to take the candy.

   As the weeks went by, the two boys became bolder and started taking more valuable things from various stores. They loved the excitement, even when they almost got caught. Tyrone began to have second thoughts and was worried about getting caught. Devon just laughed and told Tyrone that he (Devon) could outsmart anyone. Devon thought they should do something even more daring, such as breaking into someone's house to look for money.

   The teacher will ask the following questions:
   - **What influenced Devon and Tyrone to start stealing?**
   - **Why was Tyrone worried about getting caught?**
   - **Why do you think Devon wanted to try something as serious as breaking into a house?**
   - **What do you think might happen if Devon does break into a house?**
   - **How could you avoid getting involved in these kinds of activities?**

171

3. *Identify the Skill Components:* The teacher should write the skill components on sentence strips or on the chalkboard.

1. Think about what you are doing.

2. Decide why you are eager to participate.

3. Identify the consequences that may result.

4. Consider if the activity brings harm to you and/or others.

5. Consider alternative stimulating activities, if necessary.

6. Decide the consequences resulting from those.

7. Choose your activities wisely.

4. *Model the Skill:* The teacher will tell about an activity, either real or made up, that he/she finds exciting and gets a thrill from doing (skiing, sky diving, mountain climbing, hang gliding, etc.). The teacher will apply the skill components to the selected activity.

5. *Behavioral Rehearsal:*

   A. *Selection:* The teacher will select two students to role play.

   B. *Role Plays:* The two students will role play Devon and Tyrone from the introductory story, but they will use the skill components to choose a different activity. If time permits, the teacher will suggest other scenarios to be role played.

   C. *Completion:* After the role play, the teacher and class will determine if the role play was done correctly. If not, the teacher will ask the students to re-enact the role play appropriately. If yes, the role play is completed.

   D. *Reinforcers:* The teacher and class will applaud the role players and the teacher will praise them highly.

   E. *Discussion:* The teacher will ask the students the following questions:

   ▶ **What would you do to avoid getting involved in petty crimes if a friend asked you to participate?**

   ▶ **What wholesome activities can be fun and thrilling, yet do not have legal or other harmful consequence?**

6. *Practice:* The teacher will ask the students to complete the worksheet "Hang-in-There" and share their responses in class.

7. *Independent Use:* Give students copies of the worksheet "Excitement" to be completed at home and returned to school to share.

8. *Continuation:* The teacher will caution students to think before engaging in activities that could be illegal and lead to harmful or serious consequences. The teacher will motivate the children to select activities which are fun and stimulating but at the same time legal and non-violent.

Name _____ Date _____

HANG-IN-THERE

Directions: Write your answers to these questions in complete sentences; then draw a picture as instructed.

1. What is a fun and exciting activity which you like to do with a friend? Draw a picture in box #1.

   _____

   _____

   _____

   _____

2. What is an exciting activity that you know of and have not tried as yet, but would like to do? Draw a picture in box #2.

   _____

   _____

   _____

   _____

BOX #1   **BOX #2**

Name _____ Date _____

EXCITEMENT

Directions: Cut out a magazine or newspaper article about someone involved in an exciting activity not known to you but that you would like to try. If you cannot find anything, make up such an activity. Write what interests and excites you about this activity, and describe the consequences that could result and what they are. Also tell when, where and with whom you would like to do this activity. Talk to the friends you would like to have join you in this activity and describe their feelings about your suggestion, and whether they are as excited about doing it as you are.

What interests and excites me about this activity?

_____

_____

_____

_____

_____

_____

_____

When would I like to do this?

_____

_____

_____

Where would I like to do this?

_____

_____

_____

With whom would I like to do this?

_____

_____

_____

Understanding That Vandalism Is a Crime

Behavioral Objective: Youngsters will learn what vandalism is and that it is a crime and will not be tolerated in our society. The punishment is severe and can be an extended time of detention and a large fine.

Directed Lesson:

1. ***Establish the Need:*** Some youngsters lack respect for the property of others and destroy it just to have fun and to show off to their peers. Children, especially in the elementary grades, have frequently no understanding of the properties of others. They have to be told that what belongs to others is not theirs to handle, touch and willfully destroy. They must learn that if they deface the property of others it will have serious consequences for them and can change their entire life since it can lead to imprisonment with a permanent record of criminal behavior.

2. ***Introduction:*** The teacher will read the following story:

   Bobby, Dan and Michael are great friends and like to do many things together. Michael, who is the most aggressive one, usually comes up with ideas and the other two gladly accept his suggestions for having fun. One day on his way to school Michael notices that the family who lives around the corner has erected a large, new fence around the property. This wooden fence has a lot of space to be used for painting pictures, knife carving and other fun activities. This gives him an idea and he suggests to his two friends that they get some watercolor and smear it all over the fence. All three think that doing this will be great fun and they get very excited since they expect an interesting reaction from the family who owns the property and fence. They feel proud to have thought of such a stimulating activity and consider seriously doing this stunt the next day right after school. Bill, a classmate, hears them talking about their plan and tries to convince them not to do it. Can Bill succeed?

   The teacher will ask the following questions:

   ▶ **Would you participate in such an activity?**
   ▶ **If not, why not?**
   ▶ **Do you believe it is a criminal activity or just a stunt?**
   ▶ **Would it be called vandalism?**
   ▶ **What do you think are the consequences for the three boys if they execute their plan?**

3. *Identify the Skill Components:* Write the following skill components on the board or on sentence strips.

1. Plan your activities carefully.

2. Avoid causing physical and/or mental damage to anybody.

3. Respect the well-being and property of others.

4. Consider the consequence to all concerned.

5. Determine the specific immediate and future consequences upon you.

6. Make a wise decision.

4. *Model the Skill:* The teacher will role play Bill and ask three children to role play Bobby, Dan and Michael. The teacher portraying Bill will use the skill components to convince the three friends that their plan is not a wise choice for a fun activity.

5. *Behavioral Rehearsal:*

A. *Selection:* The teacher will select four groups of an appropriate number of children to role play.

B. *Role Plays:* The role plays may have the following scenarios:

- Children are punching the tires of cars in the parking lot.
- Children are throwing stones down from a bridge at cars driven in the street below.
- Children are destroying toys which do not belong to them.
- Children are tearing pages out of valuable library books.

C. *Completion:* After each role play is finished, the teacher and class will decide if the role play is correct and if the skill components were used. If not, the role play should be re-enacted with corrections; if there are no corrections needed, the role play is complete.

D. *Reinforcers:* Applause after each role play and praise from the teacher will acknowledge a job well done by the participants.

E. *Discussion:* The teacher will start the discussion by again defining what vandalism is and then ask the class about the punishment that would result for such acts. The discussion might lead to other acts of vandalism which the children have experienced and finally conclude with suggestions how to recognize that a fun activity is of criminal nature and should not be done.

6. *Practice:* The teacher will distribute the worksheet "Vandalism" and ask the children to complete the puzzle in class and discuss how the vertical words relate to vandalism.

7. *Independent Use:* The teacher will distribute the worksheet "Crime—Yes or No—" for the students to take home and return completed in one week for discussion in class.

8. *Continuation:* The teacher will reiterate the importance of respecting other people's property and will emphasize that this rule has to be followed at a young age but has to be complied with by people of all ages. The consequences of non-adherence are serious and can impact not only on the immediate lifestyle but can have a lasting effect on the person's entire life.

Name _____   Date _____

VANDALISM

Directions: Solve the crossword puzzle and you will see that the top horizontal word is "Vandalism". Start by writing in this word. The vertical lines are to be filled with words related to the act of committing vandalism and its consequences. Clues for the words in the vertical lines are:

1. Decreased in value
2. Bring charges
3. Express disapproval
4. Demolish
5. Something you do

6. Properties
7. Pertaining to crime
8. Court judgment
9. Destroy

Name _____ Date _____

VANDALISM

Answer Key

1.	2.	3.	4.	5.	6.	7.	8.	9.
D		D			B	C		D
E		E			E	R		E
V	A	N	D	A	L	I	S	M
A	C	O	E	C	O	M	E	O
L	C	U	S	T	N	I	N	L
U	U	N	T	I	G	N	T	I
A	S	C	R	V	I	A	E	S
T	E	E	O	I	N	L	N	H
E			Y	T	G		C	
D			Y	S			E	

Name _____ Date _____

CRIME—YES OR NO?

Directions: Answer the questions and describe the items below:

1. Define vandalism. _____

   _____

2. Does it hurt anybody? _____

   _____

3. Who gets hurt? _____

   _____

4. Is vandalism considered a crime? Why? _____

   _____

5. Describe possible consequences for such acts. _____

   _____

6. Write down the six skill components.

   1. _____

   2. _____

   3. _____

   4. _____

   5. _____

   6. _____

7. Make up a story in which your friends suggest that you participate in a certain "fun" activity that might be criminal. Show how you can use the skill components to decide if the activity is criminal and if your participation could have serious consequences to you. If the answer is Yes, tell if you will participate or why not and if you will try to convince your friends to abstain also from doing it and how you will talk to them. Share the story with your parent(s).

   Use the back of this page or another piece of paper to write your story.

Realizing That There Are Consequences for Criminal Actions

Behavioral Objective: Students will learn to appreciate that there is little opportunity to avoid consequences when committing crimes.

Directed Lesson:

1. **Establish the Need:** Young people are often led by their peers into thinking that there are no consequences for criminal acts. Oftentimes it is not until repeated acts are intercepted that young people realize the severity of those consequences. Young people may be assigned to detention and prison even for petty crimes, and acquire permanent crime records which affect their future education and employment opportunities.

2. **Introduction:** The teacher will ask the following questions:

    ▶ **What is crime?**
    ▶ **Why would anyone need to commit a crime?**
    ▶ **Could the consequences be harmful to one's future?**
    ▶ **What are the chances of being apprehended?**
    ▶ **Does it matter how many times the crime is committed?**

    The teacher will then read the following story:

    Carlos was a nine-year-old boy who had many friends. Some of the friends who were known to him were involved in street activities, including breaking and entering and the sale of contraband. Carlos was very much interested in purchasing a bike at the local bike shop which cost $300.00. His parents were not willing to purchase the bike for him, and he thought of many activities in which his friends were involved to provide some means for purchasing the bike. One evening as he lay in bed thinking, he came to the conclusion that it would be best for him to take his mother's credit card and purchase the bike. Within a week he was at the bike shop making his selection and was able to make the purchase using the credit card. In order to cover himself, he stored the new bike at a friend's house. Within the next month, his mother found out that he made the purchase and . . .

    Ask the students to respond to the following questions:

    ▶ **How do you think his parents responded?**
    ▶ **What consequences could he face at home and with the police?**
    ▶ **What are some suggestions to help him through the situation?**

180

3. *Identify the Skill Components:* List the following skill components on the board:

- Consider the consequences to yourself for committing a criminal act.
- Ask yourself if it is worth the risk.
- Consider the chances of being caught.
- Consider how this will affect your future.
- Make a wise choice.

4. *Model the Skill:* The teacher will model the skill by role playing Carlos in the introductory story. The teacher will select another student to portray the mother of Carlos. Using the skill components, Carlos, the teacher, will conclude that the consequences are too serious for Carlos to ever again consider such a crime.

5. *Behavioral Rehearsal:*

A. *Selection:* The teacher will select two pairs of students.

B. *Role Plays:* The teacher will ask the students to role play the following:
   - Two students discuss participating in stealing jewelry.
   - Two students discuss vandalizing a property in their neighborhood.

C. *Completion:* After each role play, the teacher will decide if the role play was done correctly and if the skill components were used appropriately. If not, the role play will be re-enacted with corrections. If yes, the role play is complete.

D. *Reinforcers:* The teacher and class will thank the role players for their participation with applause and verbal praise.

E. *Discussion:* The teacher will start the discussion by asking the students if there are any crimes that might be considered petty crimes and list them on the board. The teacher then will ask the students to indicate what they think will be the appropriate punishment for those crimes.

6. *Practice:* The teacher will distribute copies of the worksheet entitled "Consequences" and ask the students to complete the worksheet. It will be followed up with a discussion in class.

7. *Independent Use:* The teacher will distribute the worksheet "My Letter of Apology" and ask the students, with the assistance of their parents, to write a letter of apology to their parents for something that was done which may be of a criminal nature or otherwise undesirable. They are to return this within a week to share with the class.

8. *Continuation:* The teacher will utilize clips from the newspaper on a periodic basis to stress the importance of avoiding criminal activities. The articles should involve juveniles and help spark class discussion.

Name _____ Date _____

CONSEQUENCES

Directions: Let's describe some activities related to:

ACTIVITY

1. Guns, Weapons _____

2. Gangs _____

3. Drugs _____

4. Theft _____

5. Vandalism _____

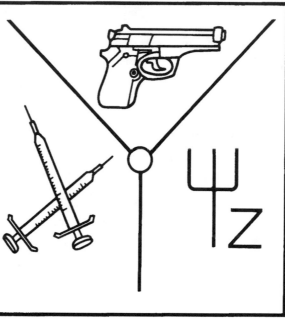

AND THE CONSEQUENCES

Consequences to You and Others:

YOU	**OTHERS**
1. _____	_____
2. _____	_____
3. _____	_____
4. _____	_____
5. _____	_____

Name _____   Date _____

MY LETTER OF APOLOGY

Dear _____,

Your _____,

Using Our Hands Appropriately

Behavioral Objective: Students will learn that their hands not only have many "positive" uses, but also can get them into trouble when they are not used correctly.

Directed Lesson:

1. **Establish the Need:** Students know that they use their hands for many good uses, such as helping, carrying, working, writing, creating, expressing, and playing. They need to understand that it is their same hands that can create problems for them when they are used for hitting, pushing, shoving, touching, stealing, using weapons, handling drugs, drinking alcohol, smoking cigarettes, vandalizing or fighting. Students need to understand how to avoid possible problem situations by learning that it is their hands that can keep them out of trouble or get them into it.

2. **Introduction:** The teacher will read the following story to the class:

   Bobby had just been arrested for shoplifting. As he sat in the back of the police car, he kept thinking about what his mother had always told him, "Those hands are going to get you into trouble if you don't use them for good things." For the first time in his life, he understood what she was trying to teach him.

   When Bobby was in school, it was his hands that got him into trouble. He was always using them to shove, push, or fight another person. He also got into a lot of trouble when he touched some girls in the wrong places.

   The only time Bobby was not in some trouble was when he was using his hands to help someone. Often he made a little money working and carrying things for people. He also loved to use his hands to catch a football and shoot basketball, and to play on a computer, especially the games on his "playstation"!

   Bobby kept thinking, "I'll never use my hands again to do something that will get me into trouble. From now on it will be just for good things." Just then the police car pulled out to take Bobby to the police station.

   The teacher will ask the class the following questions:
   - **What does Bobby's mother's saying "Those hands are going to get you into trouble if you don't use them for good things" mean to you?**
   - **Why do you think it took Bobby so long to realize what his mother was always trying to tell him about his hands?**
   - **What are some good things that you have done with your hands?**
   - **What are some bad things that you have done with your hands?**

3. ***Identify the Skill Components:*** Write the following skill components on the board or on sentence strips:

1. Analyze the many things hands can do.

2. Think before using your hands.

3. Differentiate between appropriate and inappropriate use of your hands.

4. Analyze the consequences that applying your hands can cause.

5. Determine how to create good and bad situations when applying your hands.

6. Decide how to make best use of your hands.

7. Make wise decisions.

4. ***Model the Skill:*** The teacher will "think aloud" portraying a child that is tempted to shoplift and show how the child realized, by using the skill components that shoplifting has serious consequences and thus is not worth doing.

5. ***Behavioral Rehearsal:***

A. *Selection:* The teacher will select four pairs of students to role play and ask them to use the skill components.

B. *Role Plays:* The role plays may have the following scenarios:
   - Starting a fight and ending with a handshake.
   - Enticing to vandalize a neighbor's yard.
   - Stealing candy. Yes and no.
   - Boy/girl relationship

C. *Completion:* After each role play, the teacher will decide if the role play was done correctly and if the skill components were used appropriately. If corrections are needed, the role play will be re-enacted; if not, the role play is complete.

D. *Reinforcers:* The teacher and class will thank the role players for their participation with applause and verbal praise.

E. *Discussion:* The teacher will ask the students to help in making two lists to show how hands can be used to do good and to do wrong and will ask one student to write the students' ideas on the chalkboard. These two lists might be used for a more general discussion.

6. ***Practice:*** The teacher will distribute the worksheet "Thumbs Up/Thumbs Down," for students to complete and share in class.

7. ***Independent Use:*** The teacher will distribute the worksheet "My Hands," to the class and ask students to complete and return it in one week. They will read their complete story and discuss it in class.

8. ***Continuation:*** The teacher will encourage students to follow the rules that they helped to establish for using their hands. He/she will re-emphasize the use of the skill components when various situations arise and suggest the students use their hands in ways that will help them have a successful life.

Name _____ Date _____

THUMBS UP—THUMBS DOWN

Directions: Place a thumbs up (↑) or down (↓) symbol or both symbols next to each of the following terms indicating the appropriate and inappropriate use of hands.

1. Vandalizing

2. Stealing

3. Forcing

4. Working

5. Hitting

6. Helping

7. Touching

8. Using weapons

9. Playing

10. Creating

11. Fighting

12. Cheating

13. Expressing

14. Showing

15. Carrying

16. Pushing

17. Endearing

18. Clasping

19. Greeting

20. Embracing

21. Eating

22. Breaking

23. Destroying

24. Smoking

Name _____   Date _____

MY HANDS

Directions: On this worksheet, write a short story about what you like to do with your hands and what you will not do and why. Use the back of this sheet if you need more room.

Understanding Sexual Harassment

Behavioral Objective: Students will learn and understand that sexual harassment is unwanted verbal or physical behavior of a sexual nature that interferes with a person's schoolwork performance and creates an environment that is hostile or intimidating.

Directed Lesson:

1. **Establish the Need:** Sexual harassment was once a decidedly grown-up issue. But that was before the present movement in schools that encourages strong disciplinary actions for anyone found guilty of sexually harassing another individual. In many cases, the problem exists that students don't have a real understanding of things that can be considered sexual harassment. If students learn and understand what sexual harassment is, many future problems may be eliminated.

2. **Introduction:** The teacher will read the following story to the class:

   Jonathan was the kind of boy who loved to "mess" with the girls. He was always doing something to Barbara and her best friend, Melissa. At first, the girls didn't seem to mind Jonathan, and what he did seemed harmless. But as time went on, Jonathan became more aggressive. He started trying to hug the girls and to touch their hair and clothing. Both girls continued to tell Jonathan to leave them alone; but, he continued anyway.

   Melissa and Barbara were now feeling angry and betrayed because Jonathan would not stop his actions. They got to the point that they did not want to go out on the playground after lunch, so that they could stay away from Jonathan. One day, as all the students were still in the lunchroom, Jonathan came up and tried to kiss the girls. He also threatened to beat them up if they didn't kiss him back.

   After lunch, when the girls returned to their classroom, they immediately went to their teacher and told her everything that had been going on with Jonathan. The teacher then wrote a note to the principal, who promptly came to the classroom. The principal's first words were, "Jonathan, come with me!" They both left to go to the principal's office.

   The teacher will then ask the class:

   ▶ **What do you think will happen next?**

3. **Identify the Skill Components:** The teacher will write the following skill components on a chart or on the chalkboard:

   1. Know that sexual harassment is illegal.

   2. Observe the person(s) closely.

3. Evaluate the behavior.

4. Evaluate the attitude.

5. Evaluate the problem.

6. Do not minimize the problem.

7. Ask the person(s) to stop.

8. Determine if the harassment is continuing.

9. Talk to an adult about the problem.

4. ***Model the Skill:*** The teacher will role play one of the girls from the introductory story. By using the skill components, he/she will show how to resolve the problem of sexual harassment.

5. ***Behavioral Rehearsal:***

   A. *Selection:* The teacher will select two groups of three students from the class for the role playing.

   B. *Role Plays:* The students will role play the following scenarios:

   – The first role play will involve two girls and one boy. This group will role play the introductory story by reversing the story line so that the two girls are sexually harassing the boy student. (This will demonstrate that sexual harassment occurs both ways.)

   – In the second role play, two students will sexually harass another student by making sexually oriented jokes or remarks, or using inappropriate remarks about the student's body, clothing, sexual orientation or behavior.

   C. *Completion:* After each role play, the teacher will reinforce correct behavior, identify inappropriate behaviors, and have the students re-enact the role play with corrections. If there are no corrections, the role play is complete.

   D. *Reinforcers:* The teacher and classmates will thank the role players for their participation in the role plays and will praise their performances.

   E. *Discussion:* The teacher will lead the discussion with questions such as:

   ◗ **What is the difference between verbal and physical sexual harassment?**

   ◗ **What are some feelings that are experienced by a victim of sexual harassment?**

   ◗ **What are some things you can do if you are sexually harassed?**

6. ***Practice:*** The teacher will distribute the worksheet "Sexual Harassment" for completion and discussion in class.

7. ***Independent Use:*** The teacher will distribute the worksheet entitled "Sexual Harassment Role Plays" for students to complete at home and return within one week for class discussion.

8. ***Continuation:*** The teacher will stress the point that any type of sexual harassment is against the law and should not be taking place; and if it does occur, there are consequences. The teacher will remind the students that sexual harassment can occur at any time and anywhere throughout their life. They should be reminded that if it does occur, there are a number of things that can be done to end the unwanted behavior. If everyone understands harassment and works together, sexual harassment can be eliminated.

Name _____ Date _____

SEXUAL HARASSMENT

Directions: List below five examples of behavior that could be defined as sexual harassment.

1. _____

   _____

2. _____

   _____

3. _____

   _____

4. _____

   _____

5. _____

   _____

Name _____ Date _____

Sexual Harassment Role Plays

Directions: Write the answers to each of the following role play situations.

1. John or Mary tells you a joke that contains a lot of profanity and talks about private body parts. What would you do?

   _____

   _____

   _____

   _____

   _____

   _____

2. A friend or peer tells you how much he/she likes you and wants to give you a kiss, then tells you he/she will not take "no" for an answer. What would you do?

   _____

   _____

   _____

   _____

   _____

   _____

3. _____ continues to hug you and is constantly touching your body, hair, and even your clothing. What do you do?

   _____

   _____

   _____

   _____

   _____

Respecting Dangerous Objects

Behavioral Objective: Children will learn to understand the danger of using certain objects and devices, such as knives, guns, darts, chemicals, etc. As a result, they will be better able to control their "curiosity" about such objects of "play" and avoid potential danger and bodily harm to themselves and to others.

Directed Lesson:

1. **Establish the Need:** Daily, hundreds of children are injured or maimed because of the misuse of various objects and devices found in the home and neighborhood. Specifically, guns, which are kept in numerous homes for "protection," account for many deaths of minors. Increasingly, elementary-age children bring guns to school as well as other dangerous objects such as knives and chemicals. It is important that young children understand the potential danger in the use of such objects and devices and especially learn that those devices are not permitted in school.

2. **Introduction:** The teacher will read the following story to the class:

   Two friends, Emma and Cary, both third graders, were on an errand to the corner store to get some food for lunch that their mothers had sent them for. They had been friends for a long time and were enjoying their summer vacation. On the way to the store, they were met by a boy, Mark, who was a sixth grader and had gone to the same school earlier, but had moved away. He was playing with a sharp device (an ice pick) in the dirt along the sidewalk. As boys do, he said "Hi" and invited the girls to stay and talk. They did. Soon, one of Mark's friends, Antonio, joined the group. Antonio was a belligerent sort of fellow who had a short temper and soon got into an argument with Emma. They pushed one another and he then grabbed Mark's ice pick and pushed it into her cheek. Blood began to gush from her face. She screamed, hit him, and ran back towards home with her friend. They saw a neighbor, who helped to wash the long slash, and called her mother.

   The teacher will ask the following questions:

   > **How could this violence have been avoided?**
   > **Is an ice pick an appropriate toy?**
   > **Who was at fault? Why?**

3. **Identify the Skill Components:** Write the skill components on the chalkboard or on sentence strips.

   1. Consider the danger of handling objects that can inflict bodily harm.

2. Consider the training required to operate those objects properly.

3. Determine how careful you must be to handle those objects.

4. Decide if safety is at stake.

5. Consider that safe is better than sorry.

6. Be cautious.

4. *Model the Skill:* The teacher will role play Mark and ask one student to portray Antonio. By using the skill components, the teacher will show that Mark was at fault for using the ice pick for play.

5. *Behavioral Rehearsal:*

A. *Selection:* The teacher will select four students to act out two role plays.

B. *Role Plays:* The students will enact the following scenarios:
   - A group of young people playing with knives.
   - Two students playing with firecrackers.

C. *Completion:* After each role play, the teacher will identify if the role play was done correctly and will suggest corrections if necessary. If the role play is done correctly, it is complete.

D. *Reinforcers:* The class will recognize the participants and praise the role players profusely.

E. *Discussion:* The teacher will ask the students the following questions as part of the discussion:
   - **Why would someone want to play with dangerous objects? Are the reasons "good" ones?**
   - **What are some potentially dangerous objects?**
   - **How can you avoid being tempted to play with objects that are potentially dangerous?**

6. *Practice:* The teacher will have the class members complete the worksheet "Dangerous!" After completion, the class will discuss student responses.

7. *Independent Use:* The teacher will ask the students, with a parent's help, to cut out one newspaper article describing a tragedy and paste it on the "Tragedy in Our Town" worksheet. Students will return the worksheet within one week for a follow-up discussion.

8. *Continuation:* The teacher will have the students create and maintain a bulletin board in the classroom entitled "DANGERS TO US to remind the students that dangerous objects should never be used in play or to solve conflicts.

Name _____ Date _____

DANGEROUS!

Directions: Pictured below are various objects that are potentially dangerous. Next to each object, write—after thinking about the skill components—why and how it could harm you and others.

Why and how could this object become dangerous?

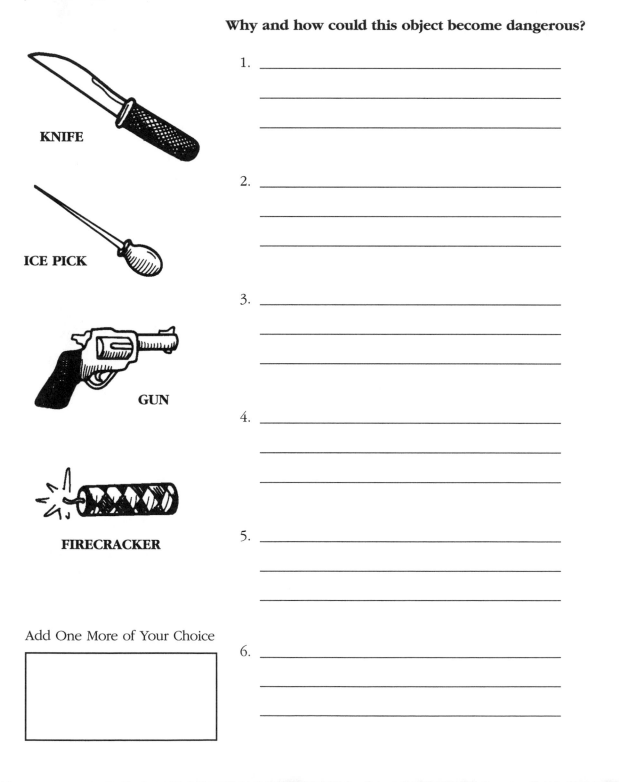

KNIFE

ICE PICK

GUN

FIRECRACKER

Add One More of Your Choice

1. _____
   _____
   _____

2. _____
   _____
   _____

3. _____
   _____
   _____

4. _____
   _____
   _____

5. _____
   _____
   _____

6. _____
   _____
   _____

Name _____ Date _____

TRAGEDY IN OUR TOWN

Directions: With the help of your parent(s) or guardian, read and cut out a newspaper article that describes what can happen when an object is misused.

Paste it below:

Now tell how, using the skill components, the tragedy could have been avoided.

_____

_____

_____

_____

_____

_____

Understanding the Consequences for Bringing Weapons to School

Behavioral Objective: Children will learn that bringing weapons, such as knives, guns and other harm-causing objects to school will have serious consequences, such as suspension and even detention, after being adjudicated in Juvenile Court. They will also learn to understand that these objects are no protection from threats by bullies but rather can cause serious injury to all involved including themselves.

Directed Lesson:

1. **Establish the Need:** It is well known that children frequently bully and sometimes threaten other children. This is often prevalent in schools where children of diverse backgrounds come together and mix with each other in work and play. Statistically, most serious bullying occurs in the elementary grades although it is also done by students in higher grades where it is often referred to as peer pressure. When children are confronted by physical and verbal threats from bullies, they become scared and think of all kinds of defenses to use against those threats. Since most children are familiar with guns, which are available in many American households, their first thought frequently is to take the father's gun to school for protection against the bully. The children are often not aware that guns are serious weapons and can cause deadly injuries to all during fights for its possession. Thus just handling and showing off a gun is more likely to be dangerous than using it for protection. Even if children know that bringing a gun to school is illegal and can have serious consequences, they believe that they can manage somehow not to be caught. Apparently they feel that the threat from the bully is worse than the idea of being caught. Youngsters have to learn to understand that guns are no protection and that they will not escape the consequences when caught with a gun in school They also will learn to realize that waving a gun in front of an adversary can result in injury and even death. Both adversaries can become victims.

2. **Introduction:** The teacher will read the following story with the class:

   Deonde has been feeling angry about a new student in the class. It seems that since Joe came to his class everything has been going wrong. Joe cuts in front of him in line and takes food off his lunch tray. Joe has been "bad mouthing" him to others in the class. When Deonde rolled his eyes at Joe for something he said, Joe threatened to beat him up after school. Thank goodness he did not see him after school. That night Deonde decided to take his father's gun to school; not that he would use it, but just to show Joe that "he better stop bothering him."

   The teacher will ask the following questions:

   ▶ **Did Deonde make a wise decision?**

196

▶ **Why did Deonde make this decision?**

▶ **Do any of you have a suggestion how Deonde could better handle the situation?**

3. *Identify the Skill Components:* Write the following skill components on the board or on sentence strips.

1. Rethink carefully the situation.

2. Determine how serious the threats are.

3. Consider your options to end the threats.

4. Consider the consequences of all options.

5. Analyze if a discussion or other peaceful means could bring closure.

6. If you need help, decide whom and when to ask.

7. Remember that all conflicts can be solved without showing off with force, such as weapons.

4. *Model the Skill:* The teacher will role play Deonde and use a "think aloud" method and the skill components to show how Deonde could solve the situation peacefully.

5. *Behavioral Rehearsal:*

   A. *Selection:* The teacher will select three groups of three students.

   B. *Role Plays:* Each group will be asked by the teacher to role play three different situations chosen and preferably experienced by one of the students in each of the groups. The student who experienced threats by others plays the main role, the second child is the one who makes the threat and the third child stands by as a trusted adult to be called for help, if needed, by the one who tries to solve the conflict in a peaceful way.

   C. *Completion:* After each role play, the teacher will decide if the role play was done correctly and if the skill components were used appropriately. If corrections are needed, the role plays will be re-enacted; if yes, the role play is complete.

   D. *Reinforcers:* The teacher and class will thank the role players for their participation with applause and verbal praise.

   E. *Discussion:* The teacher will start the discussion by asking the children how they feel about solving conflicts peacefully, without using force and objects which can cause harm. The teacher will then discuss with the entire class the harm that can be done by showing off dangerous objects even if there is not intent to use them. The discussion could also evolve around similar situations experienced by the students and how they will handle such situations from now on.

6. *Practice:* The teacher will distribute the worksheet "Play Safe—No Guns" to complete in class and discuss.

7. *Independent Use:* The teacher will distribute the worksheet "Gun/School—No" for the students to take home and return in one week for discussion in class.

8. *Continuation:* The teacher will emphasize the importance of understanding that showing off with guns, or for that matter with any other dangerous objects, is asking for serious consequences, such as injury, death, prison, detention, and possibly a wrecked future. This is true for people at any age and should be remembered throughout the entire life.

Name _____ Date _____

PLAY SAFE—NO GUNS

Directions: Complete the following sentences using the words in the box.

Guns	**Illegal**	**Dangerous**	**Angry**	**Hurt**	**Kill**

1. It is _____ to use a gun.

2. _____ are not toys.

3. It is OK to get _____.

4. I could get _____ if I use a gun.

5. I could _____ someone with a gun.

6. Bringing a gun or other weapon to school is _____.

Copy the Skill Components below:

1. _____

2. _____

3. _____

4. _____

5. _____

_____

6. _____

7. _____

_____

Tell how you will use the Skill Components:

_____

_____

_____

_____

Name _____   Date _____

GUN/SCHOOL—NO

Directions: Make up a story of a student your age who is bringing a gun to school and is caught and write it on the back of this sheet. Have your parent sign this sheet.

Answer the following questions and discuss them with your parent(s).

1. Whose gun is it? _____

2. Why did you take it? _____

3. What made you bring it to school? _____

4. What are you afraid of? _____

5. Will a gun solve the situation? _____

6. How can it solve the situation: _____

7. Do you know that a gun is a dangerous weapon? _____

8. Why is it dangerous? _____

9. Can it kill? _____

10. Whom? _____

11. Do you know the consequence for bringing a gun to school? _____

12. What are the consequences? _____

13. Are they serious? _____

14. Can you avoid the consequences? _____

15. Will they leave a mark on your record for life? _____

16. Will they hamper your educational goals? _____

17. What could you have done to solve the situation without showing off a gun? (Use the skill components.)

    _____

18. What did you learn from this lesson?

    _____

_____
Parent

SOCIAL SKILLS
FAMILY TRAINING BOOKLET

The following pages present a social skills family training booklet entitled "Partners in Social Skills: A Family Affair" preceded by a "Family Letter" that introduces the booklet and can be signed by each child. The letter provides a good way to involve parents in the social skills development program to coordinate home and classroom instruction.

NOTE: The letter and single pages of the booklet may be photocopied but only as many times as you need them for use with individual children, small groups, or an entire class. Reproduction of this material for an entire school system or for sale is strictly forbidden.

FAMILY LETTER

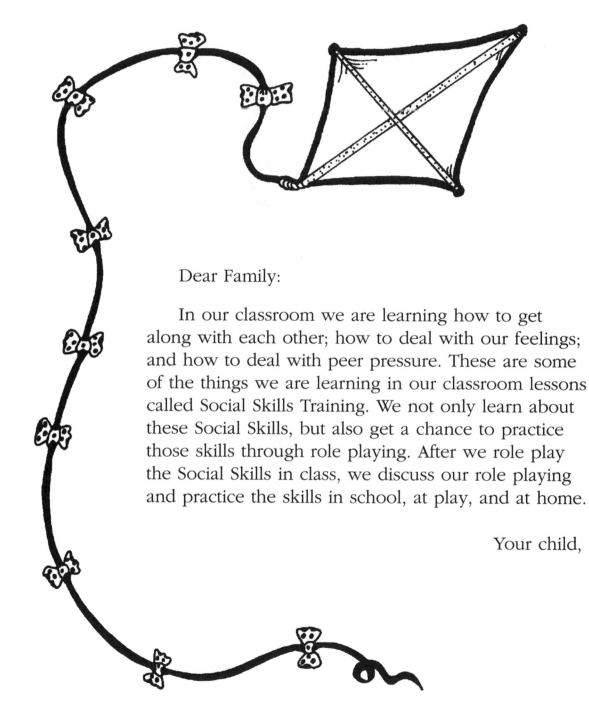

Dear Family:

In our classroom we are learning how to get along with each other; how to deal with our feelings; and how to deal with peer pressure. These are some of the things we are learning in our classroom lessons called Social Skills Training. We not only learn about these Social Skills, but also get a chance to practice those skills through role playing. After we role play the Social Skills in class, we discuss our role playing and practice the skills in school, at play, and at home.

Your child,

We Are Flying High

Partners
in
Social Skills

A Family Affair

 RUTH WELTMANN BEGUN, Editor
The Society for Prevention of Violence
with
The Center for Applied Research in Education

ACKNOWLEDGMENTS

The Founders, Trustees, Members, Friends of the Society for Prevention of Violence (SPV), and many Foundations and Corporations sponsored the writing of this social skills training booklet, "Partners in Social Skills: A Family Affair." The objective of the booklet is to acquaint the family with social skills training and how it can be used to resolve conflicts and to improve the behavior, attitude, and responsibility of the children and other family members. The booklet will help the family reinforce Social Skills Training being taught in schools and can also be used by the family to teach social skills to pre-school children.

Credit for writing the booklet belongs to a group of teachers from the Cleveland (Ohio) Public Schools who worked under the guidance of Ruth Weltmann Begun, then Executive Director of SPV. All participants utilized their expertise and considered many variations of instructional approaches and ideas until a format for the publication was agreed upon.

INTRODUCTION

"Partners in Social Skills: A Family Affair" is a Social Skills Training resource guide to be used in a family setting. Social Skills Training helps a child to gain valuable skills such as self-esteem, self-control, respect for other persons, and responsibility for one's own actions. Such skills are very important for good family relationships, solid learning in school, and success all through life.

Some schools now offer Social Skills training in their classrooms. For many children this supports what they are already learning at home. For many others, school is where they start to learn such skills. Many families today have single parents, or have two parents who both work, or have step-parents due to divorce and remarriage. All these changes put stress on families, and make parenting more challenging than in the past.

Today, the average child watches several hours of television each day, often without a parent or other adult present. TV scenes of violence or other harmful conduct can easily misguide young children.

This guide is designed to help parents in several ways:

1. To introduce Social Skills Training to parents, and show them how this is already taught in some schools.

2. To present some Social Skills Training activities that can be done at home.

3. To encourage parents to apply this training with all of their children, even preschoolers.

4. To remind parents that, no matter how much they may sometimes doubt it, *they* are the most important teachers in their children's lives.

The love, example, and guidance of parents and other adult family members can indeed make the difference for a child. He or she can learn, with their help, to respect others, make wise decision, avoid violence, and become a successful and productive citizen as an adult.

Along the way, practicing the Social Skills included here should help the family enjoy a happier and less stressful home life.

THE SOCIAL SKILLS SONG

(Tune: "Mary Had a Little Lamb")

WE CAN USE OUR SOCIAL SKILLS
SOCIAL SKILLS, SOCIAL SKILLS
WE CAN USE OUR SOCIAL SKILLS
AS WE SPREAD OUR GOOD WILL

EVERY DAY IN EVERY WAY
EVERY WAY, EVERY WAY
EVERY DAY IN EVERY WAY
OUR CHARACTER WE BUILD

S elf-image improved
O nly giving compliments
C ompleting tasks
I gnoring distractions
A nger dealt with
L ess aggression

S eatwork and homework done
K eep following classroom rules
I gnoring teasing
L eave a troublesome situation
L earning to accept consequences
S taying out of fights

TABLE OF CONTENTS

(R) = reproducible

OUR FAMILY SOCIAL SKILLS
TRAINING CHECKLIST

Directions: Please fill out this checklist as a family before starting to read this book. Answer the way your family really feels by filling in the faces. There are no right or wrong answers.

This will help your family understand the need to practice Social Skills Training in your home.

Almost Always ☺		Sometimes 😐		Almost Never ☹

		Almost Always	Sometimes	Almost Never
1.	Do we understand and follow when directions are given?	☺	😐	☹
2.	Do we know and follow the rules in our home?	☺	😐	☹
3.	Do we listen to adults in authority?	☺	😐	☹
4.	De we finish our household jobs?	☺	😐	☹
5.	Do we take our finished homework to school the next day?	☺	😐	☹
6.	Do we finish our housework even when others are not doing their share?	☺	😐	☹
7.	Do we keep busy and quiet when waiting for our parent's attention?	☺	😐	☹
8.	Do we find something quiet and helpful to do when we have free time?	☺	😐	☹
9.	Do we deal with anger in a way that won't hurt others?	☺	😐	☹
10.	Do we stay in control when somebody teases us?	☺	😐	☹
11.	Do we think of ways other than fighting to handle our problems?	☺	😐	☹
12.	Do we avoid fighting when someone threatens or hits us?	☺	😐	☹
13.	Do we accept the consequences when we do something we shouldn't?	☺	😐	☹
14.	Do we tell others that we like something nice about them or do something nice for them?	☺	😐	☹
15.	Do we say and do nice things for ourselves when we have earned it?	☺	😐	☹

HELPFUL HINTS FOR USING THIS BOOK

1. Set aside quiet time and space.

2. Involve all family members.

3. Discussions should be friendly, positive and open.

4. Listen to each member's comments.

5. Criticism should be done in a positive and peaceful way.

6. All family members should work on being good role models.

BE A ROLE MODEL FOR YOUR CHILD

- Let your child see you read. Visit the library with your child on a regular basis. At home, provide a quiet, well-lighted space for your child to study and read.

- Don't leave your children alone for long periods of time. Let your child know where and how to reach you. Leave your child with a happy feeling.

- Use kind and supportive words with your child. Unkind words can hurt as much as, or even more than, physical punishment.

- When resolving disputes or conflicts in the family, do your best to stay calm and in control of yourself.

- Beginning with yourself, make all family members responsible for keeping themselves and the house clean.

- Show your child how to "just say no" by your *own* saying no to drugs and other harmful activities.

- Remember that your child is learning from you, not only when you are telling him or her what to do, but *all* the time, by your example.

FAMILY ACTIVITY PAGE

Toot Your Own Horn

Write or draw five things you can do well at home, at work, at school or at play.

FOURTEEN SELECTED SOCIAL SKILLS

The following pages contain fourteen selected Social Skills that have been taken from the "Social Skills Curriculum Activities Library" published by The Center for Applied Research in Education. Each skill is followed by skill activities. It is suggested that these activities can be done with all the family to develop the skill.

FAMILY SOCIAL SKILLS

Skill No. 1:   *Giving Compliments:*

Compliments mean saying something nice that makes someone else feel good.

Do these skill activities with your family:

1. Select someone to give a compliment.
2. Think of a compliment that is pleasing and truthful.
3. Say the compliment in a pleasant way.

Skill No. 2:   *Asking Permission:*

Permission means giving consent.

Do these skill activities with your family.

1. Ask if you may borrow something.
2. Do not take the item if the answer is no.
3. If given permission, be careful with the item and return it in good condition.
4. Say "thank you."

Skill No. 3:   Disciplinary Strategies:

Discipline is training and conduct that develops self-control.

Do these skill activities with your family.

1. Develop rules and consequences for family members.
2. Encourage all members to follow the rules.
3. Evaluate and change the rules when needed.

Skill No. 4:   Respect for Others:

Respect means to be kind and courteous to others

Do these skill activities with your family.

1. Use the words "may I" when asking someone for something.
2. Use "please" and "thank you" when asking and receiving help.
3. Practice using these word often.

Skill No. 5: Using Self-Control:

Self-control is remaining calm under stress and excitement.

Do these skill activities with your family.

1. Stop and think about the situation that was causing stress to you and made you excited.
2. Count to ten while trying to remain calm.
3. Decide what you will do next.
4. Do it in a peaceful manner.

Skill No. 6: Improving Self-Image:

Self-image is how you see yourself.

Do these skill activities with your family.

1. Think of something you like about yourself.
2. Share it with your family members.
3. Discuss more ways you are special.

Skill No. 7: Expressing Feelings:

Some feelings words are: happy, sad, angry, embarrassed, depressed, proud, guilty, frustrated, and many more.

Do these skill activities with your family.

1. Listen to the tone of voice, watch facial expressions and body gestures to understand the feelings in a message.
2. Ask the speaker if you understood his or her feelings correctly.

Skill No. 8:   Accepting Consequences:

Accepting the results of one's own actions without complaining.

Do these skill activities with your family.

1. Decide if what you did was wrong.
2. Admit what you did was wrong.
3. Try to explain why you did it.
4. Accept the punishment without complaint.

Skill No. 9:   Reacting to Failure:

Failure is an unsuccessful attempt to achieve a goal.

Do these skill activities with your family.

1. Discuss what it means to fail.
2. Decide why you failed.
3. Accept the failure.
4. Make a new plan to avoid making any similar mistakes.

Skill No. 10:   Setting Goals:

Goals are plans of action which can be achieved.

Do these skill activities with your family.

1. Thinking about things that need to be done at home or school.
2. Choose a goal and decide how it can be reached.
3. Reward yourself when you have reached your goal.

Skill No. 11:   Dealing with Prejudice:

Prejudice is caused because of differences existing between people which are not acceptable to you.

Do these skill activities with your family.

1. Discuss individual physical differences.
2. Discuss likenesses.
3. Treat everyone equally and with respect.
4. Discuss positive qualities and include everyone in your activities.

Skill No. 12:   Dealing with Anger:

Everyone gets angry but anger must be resolved in a peaceful, verbal and non-physical manner.

Do these skill activities with your family.

1. Stop and think about how you feel.
2. Think of non-threatening ways to handle your anger.
3. Choose an action that will resolve the conflict.
4. If there is no other choice, walk away.

Skill No. 13:   Dealing with Peer Pressure:

Peer Pressure means that pressure is being strongly forced on you by friends, to do something you might or might not want to do. You might decide that what they want you to do is right or wrong..

We all have friends that we adore
And that they like us we are sure
We know they're friends because they care
We know they're friends because they're fair
Then there are others that are fakes
We must watch out for our own sakes
They'll try to get us to do much wrong
So with these people we don't belong
Say no to things you see are bad
And for yourself you'll be glad
Friends won't ask us to misbehave
If you say no, we'll rave and rave.

After reading the poem do these skill activities with your family.

1. Decide if what your friends want you to do is right or wrong. If it seems wrong, consider the consequences. Don't join activities which hurt, damage others, or yourself. If caught you might be imprisoned and penalized. Say "NO" to drugs, alcohol and early sex. They will harm you.

2. Make a decision you can live with.

3. Think of other activities the group could participate in that are acceptable.

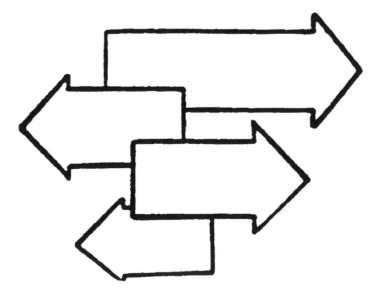

Skill No. 14:   *Problem Solving:*

There are many ways to solve a problem and make a decision. All possibilities should be considered to find the best solution.

Do these skill activities with your family.

1. State the problem and list ways it can be solved.
2. Select and try one of the choices.
3. If it does not work try another solution until you find the best one.

FAMILY ACTIVITY PAGE

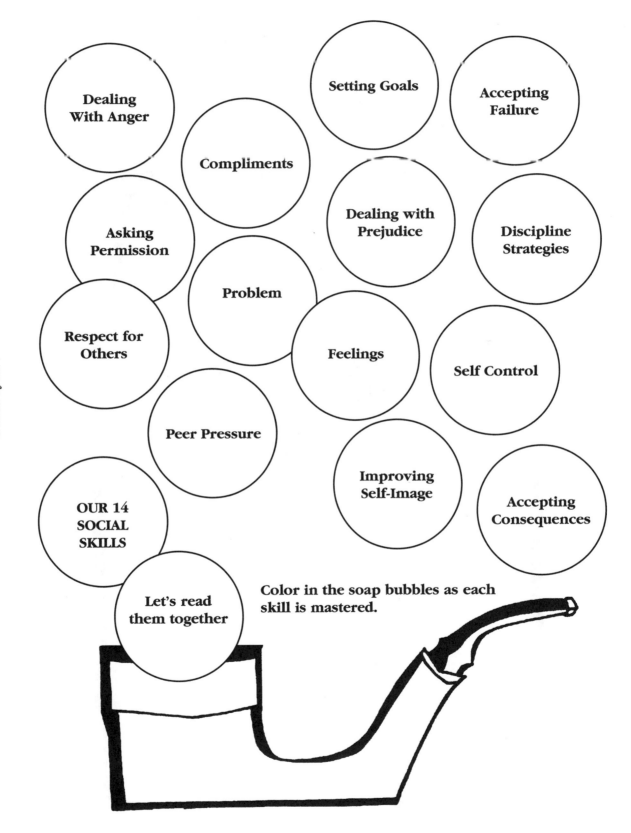

Dealing With Anger

Setting Goals

Accepting Failure

Compliments

Asking Permission

Dealing with Prejudice

Discipline Strategies

Problem

Respect for Others

Feelings

Self Control

Peer Pressure

Improving Self-Image

OUR 14 SOCIAL SKILLS

Accepting Consequences

Let's read them together

Color in the soap bubbles as each skill is mastered.

"MIRROR, MIRROR" POEM

Read the poem. Think of someone to compliment. Draw their picture and write the compliment underneath.

Mirror, mirror on the wall
Give a compliment, and that's not all
Make it nice and make it kind
A deserving person is not hard to find.

FAMILY ACTIVITY PAGE, CERTIFICATE

Use this certificate to reward family members for proper use of social skills.

BEAR-R-Y GOOD FOR YOU!

NAME:

SKILLS:

DATE:

FAMILY ACTIVITY PAGE, CERTIFICATE

KEEP MOVING YOU ARE LOOKING GOOD!

NAME:

SKILLS:

DATE:

Use this certificate to reward family members for proper use of social skills.

FAMILY TIME—GROUP DISCUSSIONS

Directions to Family: Please set aside ten to fifteen minutes daily to discuss the following questions with family members. During the family discussion be sure to listen to each other. Every family member should be encouraged to give input. Refer to the Social Skills listed in this book.

1. What Social Skills did you learn today?

2. What Social Skills did you use today?

3. What Social Skills did we use within our home?

4. What Social Skills did you use in solving a personal conflict?

5. Did you use courtesy words like "please" and "thank you" when requesting and receiving assistance?

6. What did you do today that made you feel proud?

7. What assignments including household chores did you complete today?

8. Were there any consequences that were difficult for you to accept?

9. How did you show respect for someone today?

10. Did you compliment someone today? How did this make you feel? How did this make the other person feel?

11. Which Social Skill will be our goal to work on tomorrow?

WHAT MAKES YOU HAPPY?

Directions to Family: It is suggested that all family members take part in this activity. Each member may list or draw three things that make them happy. (You may want to use additional paper.)

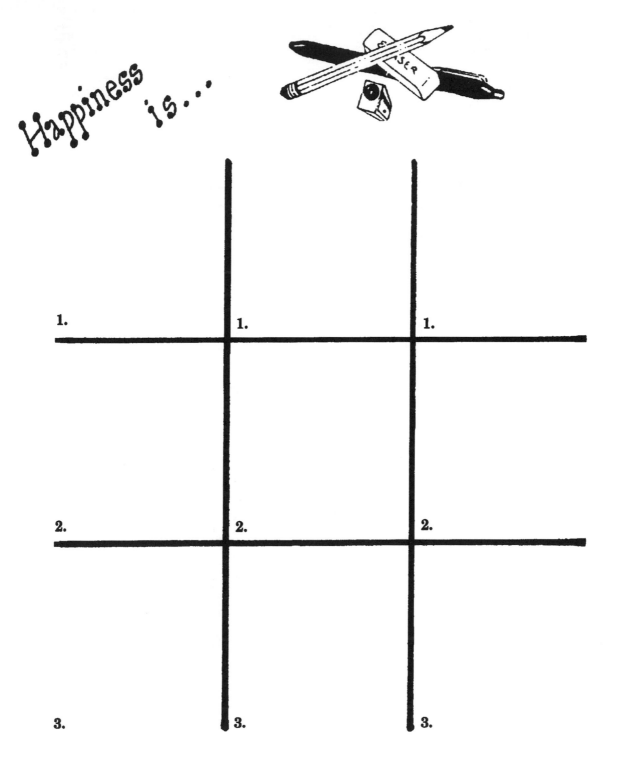

PARENT-TEACHER COMMUNICATION

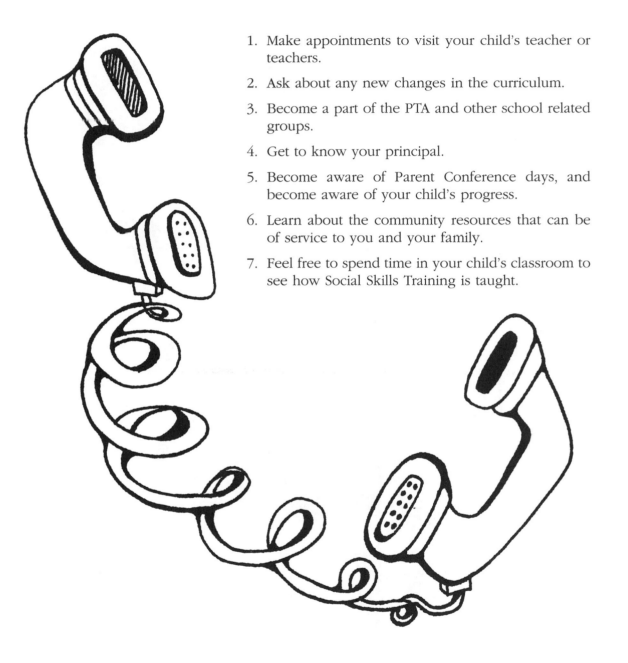

1. Make appointments to visit your child's teacher or teachers.

2. Ask about any new changes in the curriculum.

3. Become a part of the PTA and other school related groups.

4. Get to know your principal.

5. Become aware of Parent Conference days, and become aware of your child's progress.

6. Learn about the community resources that can be of service to you and your family.

7. Feel free to spend time in your child's classroom to see how Social Skills Training is taught.

COLORING ACTIVITY PAGE, PART I

After working on social skills, Mr. And Mrs. Mouse took their family on a cookout.

COLORING ACTIVITY PAGE, PART II

Tommy Mouse and his sister were happy about the cookout. They watched their manners and talked about what fun they had making it a family affair. They all agreed to work, play, and respect one another. How about your family members?

OUR FAMILY SOCIAL SKILLS
TRAINING CHECKLIST

Directions: Please fill out this reaction as a family, when you have completed this book. This may be used to help your family better understand what Social Skills need to be reinforced within the home.

Almost Always ☺	Sometimes 😐	Almost Never ☹

		Almost Always	Sometimes	Almost Never
1.	Do we understand and follow when directions are given?	☺	😐	☹
2.	Do we know and follow the rules in our home?	☺	😐	☹
3.	Do we listen to adults in authority?	☺	😐	☹
4.	De we finish our household jobs?	☺	😐	☹
5.	Do we take our finished homework to school the next day?	☺	😐	☹
6.	Do we finish our housework even when others are not doing their share?	☺	😐	☹
7.	Do we keep busy and quiet when waiting for our parent's attention?	☺	😐	☹
8.	Do we find something quiet and helpful to do when we have free time?	☺	😐	☹
9.	Do we deal with anger in a way that won't hurt others?	☺	😐	☹
10.	Do we stay in control when somebody teases us?	☺	😐	☹
11.	Do we think of ways other than fighting to handle our problems?	☺	😐	☹
12.	Do we avoid fighting when someone threatens or hits us?	☺	😐	☹
13.	Do we accept the consequences when we do something we shouldn't?	☺	😐	☹
14.	Do we tell others that we like something nice about them or do something nice for them?	☺	😐	☹
15.	Do we say and do nice things for ourselves when we have earned it?	☺	😐	☹

GUIDELINES FOR CARING PARENTS

I. How your children learn to act depends on what they are taught—and YOU are their most important teacher.

II. Your children will learn more from watching what you do than from listening to what you say to do.

III. Remember that you were once a child, and treat your children with patience and understanding.

IV. Be fair, be consistent, and respect your children as you would have them respect you.

V. Stay close to your children, but give them room to learn from their own experiences and to think for themselves.

VI. Show your children things in life that are beautiful, and show that you appreciate these things.

VII. Love your children with all your heart, your mind and your strength, and everything else will follow.

Dedicated to all family members who accept the challenge of helping each other develop into mature, healthy, stable, responsible and productive citizens.